Stop Overthinking!

A Practical Guide to Rewire Your Brain, Defeat Negative Thinking, and Take Control of Your Life

By: Devin White

ALL RIGHTS RESERVED

No part of this book may be reproduced, stored in a retrieval system, or transmitted in any form or by any means, electronic, mechanical, photocopying, recording, scanning, or otherwise, without the prior written permission of the publisher.

Limit of Liability/Disclaimer of Warranty: the publisher and the author make no representations or warranties with respect to the accuracy or completeness of the contents of this work and specifically disclaim all warranties, including without limitation warranties of fitness for a particular purpose. No warranty may be created or extended by sales or promotional materials. The advice and strategies contained herein may not be suitable for every situation. This work is sold with the understanding that the publisher is not engaged in rendering medical, legal or other professional advice or services. If professional assistance is required, the services of a competent professional person should be sought. Neither the publisher nor the author shall be liable for damages arising herefrom. The fact that an individual, organization or website is referred to in this work as a citation and/or potential source of further information does not mean that the author or the publisher endorses the information the individuals, organization or website may provide or recommendations they/it may make. Further, readers should be aware that websites listed on this work may have changed or disappeared between when this work was written and when it is read.

Table of Contents

Preface 1

Introduction 5

Chapter 1: What Are You Worried About? 7

Chapter 2: Stop Trying to Impress 24

Chapter 3: How Overthinking Can Cause Physical Pain and Illness... 34

Chapter 4: 5 Reasons You May Be Overthinking Things 47

Chapter 5: 10 Ways to Keep Yourself in Check 65

Chapter 6: The Power of Self-Love............................... 88

Chapter 7: Daily Tools to Help Clear Your Mind and Get Rid of Overthinking For Good.. 93

Chapter 9: Flip It and Reverse It 108

Chapter 10: The Hard Truths....................................... 120

Chapter 11: Therapy Isn't as Scary as It Sounds 132

Chapter 12: What Other People Are Doing 135

Preface

I am 36 years old with three kids and because I had my first at 18 and the next two closely following behind, I am usually the youngest mom at school events or sporting games. I have adult ADHD and although it may be the cause of my need to control things, constantly be on the move, and always cleaning, organizing, and rearranging things on a regular basis, it may also contribute to my feeling like I don't fit in. Or maybe, I really just DON'T FIT IN. However, as I explore more into this feeling and the way I see things, it is becoming clearer that I tend to purposely make myself *not* fit in.

I tend to love too much and care too often. I have a temper and will defend whatever it is I feel is right. I have had depression, anxiety, and a miscarriage that exacerbated the already boiling pot of emotions bubbling inside me. (That one took a while to heal.) I have had good relationships, bad relationships, toxic ones, and everything in between. I have been with the same amazing, loving, and caring man for 18 years, but it hasn't always been easy. We have gone through a lot of ups and downs that stemmed from PTSD, anxiety, depression, and other mental health issues that come with abusive childhoods (not mine, my childhood was about as good as it gets), getting pregnant at 18, and not having much when starting off in life at such a young age.

I am writing this book because I know I am not the only one who struggles. I know that other people go through these very issues, day after day. Nobody ever wants to talk about it though. It's as if being overwhelmed and sad is something that should be kept a secret. But this is life, and life is hard. What makes it harder is when you think you're alone and you think too much. When you allow yourself to let all your problems and negative thoughts swirl around in your head, constantly making you want to hide, it is time to let go of this need to be spectacular and this need to fit in. Not wanting anyone around you to see you're struggling or drowning. This is me, or was me. I am working on it. But it's nothing I am ashamed of anymore; I am ready to say it's okay to just be me.

I used to have full blown anxiety attacks allowing people to come over to my house. Even my family…on holidays. It's not that it was ever "dirty." (Even though having a family at a real young age put us in a position of not being able to afford much in the way of decor when we purchased our first home.) I was always on the move. I would rearrange the rooms weekly making sure the house was cleaned from top to bottom and crack to crack. But when someone would come over, I would panic, I would notice a spot on the refrigerator, or my kids' fingerprints stained into the paint on the wall. I was an emotional mess noticing every single soiled area of my home the entire time. Did they notice it? I have no idea; if they did, they never mentioned it. But because I knew it was there, I was ashamed and embarrassed. I started to avoid having people come to my house and would even go out of my way to meet with someone somewhere else with every excuse in the book because I hated the idea of going through the feelings I got when people would enter the house.

My house is not the only thing that made me feel that way. I was embarrassed by my vehicles, the clothes the kids and I would wear, even the way the lawn looked on the days we didn't have time to mow. Keep in mind, my vehicles were always fairly nice, the kids were always clean and dressed in popular clothing brands, and no one cared or complained about our yard. None-the-less, I stayed far away from conversations and social gatherings as much as I possibly could.

I'm laying this all out for you in this book because I know you have done the same things. You are reading this book because you were ashamed of yourself in some way or another, embarrassed by who you are, or saddened because of who you are not. You have decided that you're not good enough. I'm hoping with this book, I can help you see how wrong you are.

It hasn't even been a full-year journey yet for me, and I am still working on myself, and I may be a work in progress for the rest of my life. But I have finally found my reason to accept me for who I am, and slowly I have started to love that person. I accept me, flaws and all. In this journey, I have found that I have made myself the outsider in so many situations, not the people around me. I was so afraid that I didn't fit in or I wasn't wanted. I wouldn't try to connect with others. I even had myself convinced I wasn't good enough to be associating with some of these people.

Since I started trying to reinvent myself, I have started to notice that I actually do fit in, and I can have a good time in a group of people. If you can believe it, people did like me. The problem wasn't other people and what they thought of me. It was what I thought of myself. I was my biggest critic and super judgmental. I look back on my life and can't believe the opportunities I missed out on, and the possible friends I could have had. I'm hoping that if just one person reads this book and gets helpful information from it, then it was well worth the time. There is no one in the world who should think so negatively about themselves that they keep themselves from living. I was worth the work, you are too.

Introduction

It's safe to say we all do it. However, if you are reading this book, then it's probably because you do it way too much, and it's negatively impacting your life. It's hard *not* to overthink things these days when everything we say and do can be re-played for us at any given moment. We are forced to worry about how we look, how our kids look, or if our landscaping looks good enough from the side of the road. Did we say the right things on the conference call yesterday? Was the last text sent to our friend written in the correct tone? Did the hilarious joke we told at the office Christmas party sound ridiculous? There is nothing about our daily lives that we are not constantly replaying in our heads, wondering if it was good enough or if we are messing it all up.

The good news is that you can stop this constant urge to second guess yourself. You can stop yourself from overthinking. All you have to do is rewire your brain to allow yourself to believe you are good enough. Do *you* like what *you* are wearing? Did *you* have a good time at the Christmas party? These are the questions you should be asking yourself. Why? Because you are the only one who matters when it comes to self-love, self-respect, and self-reassurance.

If you ask the experts, they will tell you anxiety is at the core of overthinking. What is the biggest culprit for anxiety? Too much stress. Sadly, these days, there is no way around stress. We cannot ignore the world-wide Covid-19 pandemic, and I am sure we can all agree that it has negatively affected each and every one of us more than ever. If you're not worried about your own health, you are worried about your friends and families. You worry about job security, mortgage payments, health insurance. Money was the root of all evil before COVID-19 and is now so twice as much.

We have written this book for YOU, to help YOU get a grip on your self-doubts, your reasoning for feeling less than or inadequate when around others. Are you fed up with never thinking you fit in, thinking others are talking about you, or worse, laughing at you behind your back? Then let us help you. Let us teach you ways to stop the overthinking and self-doubt once and for good. Read these chapters thoroughly and carefully. You chose this title for a reason. You are ready for a change. You are ready to become a better person, a happier person. Now you just need help getting there. Lucky for you, we have done all the work. So, sit down, take notes, and get ready to change your life.

Chapter 1: What Are You Worried About?

Before you can stop yourself from thinking about why you are not good enough, you must understand where these thoughts are coming from. This can be very hard for so many people, facing themselves in a way they have never done before. For many, it's more comfortable to think everything you are doing is wrong, rather than allowing yourself to believe you are just as good as the rest of the world.

Falling into this hole of comparing yourself to everyone around you can be exhausting and it can consume you. There needs to be a time you realize you can't be like everyone else, simply because no one can. Take a look in the mirror, tell yourself you are good enough. Not just good enough, tell yourself you are exceptional, beautiful, and resilient. Seriously, you need to do this. You need to face yourself, your very own demons, and yell at them! Let them know you are done feeling bad! Chances are good you will feel silly doing this, because you either don't believe the words you are saying, or that overthinking has taken over again; and even though you are sitting alone in your room, you feel ridiculous and think others could be peering in laughing at you. That's okay, that's what we are here for. To get those negative thoughts out of your head for good.

So, what is it that stops you from thinking you are less than amazing? Why are you so afraid of believing in yourself? It's time to reflect. Take out a notebook and write a list of all your flaws. You should write down every tiny thing you tell yourself throughout the day that can make you feel like you don't fit in or you are failing at something. For now, just jot down anything that you think of. From something as small as not painting your toenails knowing you will be wearing open-toed shoes to work the next day, to choosing a college that wasn't right for you and you can't join in on the dorm party days, to conversations that pop up when you are in a group of your peers. Write it all. Take in how every single one of them makes you feel as you are scribbling them onto the page. This won't be as effective if you are typing the words on a tablet or asking Alexa to put it into a note tab for you. Take out a piece of paper and pen and feel the words. Acknowledge why you are so emotional when you write them down. Understand what it is that makes you feel so negatively about yourself.

Keep this list with you for a few days. Put it in your purse, your back pocket, your wallet. Put it on the dashboard of your car or slide it into your briefcase. Write down the events throughout the day and the things that made you feel any type of self-doubt. You will encounter situations that you never realized caused you so much anxiety. Writing these things down will help you realize where you are struggling the most.

After you have done this for a few days, take the notebook out, and categorize them.

- Relationships- Family, friends, colleagues, employees, employers, teachers
- Interactions- Writing an email, talking on the phone, zoom calls, group meetings
- Daily tasks- Cleaning, driving, cooking, getting dressed, parenting
- Emotional- Separation, trust, love, empathy, hate

Where do you rank the highest (have the most items)? That's where you need to start in your journey of becoming a better you.

Relationships

Do you come home from work feeling so tired you can barely move? Do you throw chicken nuggets and tater-tots into the oven as you hop in the shower, giving yourself some "you" time before homework and bedtime routines? Do you feel guilty for not getting all six food groups from the food pyramid onto your child's plate? Do you think your partner is judging you because you didn't spend an hour in front of the stove cooking up a four-course meal? Do you think somehow your mother-in-law is going to find out and tell you how poor of a parent you are?

Let it go. Are your children fed? Did you get to take a shower so you're not going to bed feeling grimy from a long day? Did you do what needed to be done to end the day without collapsing from exhaustion? Well, then you did great.

Do you feel guilty your tater-tots didn't really count as a vegetable? Solve the problem with an apple for a bedtime snack. Make yourself feel better by throwing carrots into your children's lunch boxes the next day. Give yourself a way to rectify the situation in your brain to stop from beating yourself up over the smallest details. Allow yourself to understand "perfect" is not the same look on everyone. It is unique to you and your circumstances. You can be perfect when doing the exact opposite of your best friend, mother, or the local grocery store owner.

This is the perfect time to tell you it could be worse. You aren't sending your kids to bed hungry, and you are not telling them to fend for themselves, and you are not giving them ice cream, telling them to eat up. So, who cares what your mother-in-law thinks? Is your spouse the one judging? They have two hands as well, surely they also know how to use the stove. If they are not happy with what you provided, then that is their problem to deal with, not yours. You cannot please everyone. Stop trying to.

Interactions

Does your stress lie within your daily interactions outside of the home? Going to work, hailing a cab, getting meat from the deli? Sometimes social anxiety can change who we are on the inside, fearing that people around us are constantly judging. True, some probably are; however, most are not. Your average store clerk couldn't care less what you are wearing or how you say thank you. Just like you, they are trying to make it through their day so they can go home and relax.

Are you worried you look like a bad employee, neighbor, or parent? Chances are good no one is judging you, but IF they are, should you really care? Is that going to change what is really important at the end of the day? I'd bet a hundred dollars that a brain fog during a work meeting, or forgetting about parent-teacher conferences, won't end up in the local news the next day. You can reschedule your meeting with your child's teacher, or have the appointment over the phone, and you likely have the opportunity to email your co-workers whatever it was you forgot as soon as it comes back to you.

In these types of situations, you have to stop singling yourself out. You are not the only person to forget things, important or not. Another downside to stress and anxiety is forgetfulness. We are all doing it and 90% of your peers understand. Whether you want to believe it or not, they not only understand but would probably be more than happy to help you out wherever needed if you would just ask.

If your negative thoughts tend to come to you during social interaction, you need to work on how you feel about yourself before you even leave your house. Do not dress to impress anyone other than yourself. Feel good before you even walk out that door. If that means some stilettos and hoop earrings, go for it. If it's throwing on a teeth-whitening strip while you're combing your mustache, YES. If it is walking out the door in a tracksuit and bed head, have at it. Whatever it is you do to get yourself motivated for the day, do it, and do it for you.

If you are out and about and uncomfortable physically, then you are setting yourself up to be uncomfortable, emotionally and mentally. If you can't walk in stilettos, you will not stop feeling self-conscious that people are giggling about a misstep or wobbling every time you get up from your desk. You are also going to give yourself a reason to constantly be overthinking your choices every time you move. This will make you feel bad that you can't walk in stilettos, and it will make you feel self-conscious around those who can. Remember the best way to feel confident is to feel comfortable in your own skin.

Do you really want to feel confident in four-inch heels? If that is something you want, want it for YOU; don't wear them out of the house until you have practiced walking in them. Until you can rock those heels on any surface the Lord has bestowed upon us. Once you know how to feel comfortable in them, you will exude confidence when you are wearing them out in public.

Hopefully, you understand this doesn't only apply to shoes. Hopefully, your take-away from this is to solve your problems in private, so you can feel 100% in public. That applies to white teeth, a well-fitted tracksuit, or any other thing you do to prepare to exit the house and walk into a world full of independent styles, thinking, and communication. Confidence in yourself is going to help you feel confident when interacting with everyone else.

Daily tasks

Do you find yourself wishing you had hit the gym that morning, but couldn't get out of bed? Is your house a mess because of soccer practice, eight hours at the office, and endless laundry? Do you find that you will not let your friends come into your home because you are terrified they are going to judge the toys from one end of the house to the other, or the overflow of dishes spewing out of the sink?

Sadly, these are all things you cannot get away from. You must go to work or you can't pay the bills, laundry will pile up because that's what it does, and driving back and forth to...well, anywhere, including soccer practice. And no matter how hard we can wish for more time, 24 hours is all we get. Let go of trying to do it all.

Adults in every stage of life try to fit it all in. Parents try to juggle work, sports, and school. College students try to study, work after class, and keep up with friends. The world is a busy place, and it just keeps getting busier. Everyone is striving for perfection, and it's time for someone to say STOP. Perfectionists aren't real, getting it all done is not possible, and doing what is most important to you and your family is all you should worry about.

Time for that notebook and pen again. Now, write out a list of your daily *to-do's*. Every single thing. Wake up, brush your teeth, start the coffee pot, pull the kids out of the bed, etc. All the way to go to bed. Now, when you are in bed, write down everything you wanted to get done and didn't. Think about how it makes you feel. Do you feel worse knowing you have dirty dinner plates still sitting in your sink, or do you feel better knowing they are still sitting there because you watched your son score his first goal in soccer?

Prioritize your time to help you stop thinking about how much you didn't get to. Get a better understanding of where you are lacking and how you can turn it around. If your dishes sitting in the sink are that big of an issue for you, prioritize them. Wash them as they come in so they can't pile up. Clean them up after soccer while your child is taking a bath. Is your child old enough to do the dishes?

Let it go. If you are obsessed with the dishes because you are terrified someone will come to the house and judge you, that's not a good enough reason to stress yourself out trying to find time to get them done. Remember this book is to teach you how to be happy with yourself. Not how to make time to be perfect and make others believe you ARE perfect. If you can live the rest of your night peacefully knowing no one will be coming over and seeing those dishes in your sink, then leave them there. Why? Because they are not a top priority to you; they are top priority to how you feel others see you. That's what we are trying to get away from.

Emotional

This is the hardest one to recognize and change. You must be willing to open up and allow yourself to feel the pain to know what is causing it. No one wants to look directly into the eyes of the monster that stalks them each day. It's easier to tell yourself monsters aren't real and choose to ignore them. Because emotional issues cannot be seen, it's easy to pretend they are not actually there. These are the little internal voices that eat at you until you feel completely lost.

The sad truth is we are living in a world where we all have to wear a thick layer of skin. We are taught to be strong and not show our emotions. When men cry, they are acting like girls, when girls cry they are acting like babies, and when babies cry we are told to let them cry it out and not acknowledge they are upset. There is an endless cycle of ignoring emotions from the moment we are born. That doesn't mean the pain isn't still there, it just means you have to keep it bottled inside. Maybe that has something to do with the increase in stress and depression these days.

As I write this, we are in the middle of a terrible pandemic that is wreaking havoc all over the world—people are unable to see their loved ones, hug their friends, or enjoy traveling with their families. The human race is a social species; we need to be with others. Social distancing has created an uncomfortable and painful gap in our lives that is causing emotional turmoil. Unfortunately, there is not much we can do to change that right now. We cannot stop social distancing. So, like any other emotional issue, it's time to learn how to deal with it.

Do not allow yourself to believe the crazy talk that makes others believe showing your emotions is wrong. You will never be able to heal or get past any problems you have if you are constantly covering them up. Feel your emotions, write them down, learn where they are coming from, and take charge of them.

Trust

Do you struggle with trusting the people you interact with on a daily basis? The people who you rely on for comfort, security, and happiness? Has someone hurt you in the past? Did you trust someone close and they betrayed you? If this is the case, you must forgive. Easier said than done, I know, but without forgiving the situation you will never get past the pain.

I am not saying you must forgive and forget; if never talking to that person again helps you move on, then do it. Forgive the situation though; forgive yourself for allowing the situation to take place. If you are one of those people who tend to blame yourself for not noticing what was happening to you when it was happening, allow yourself to say it's okay. The past is the past, you cannot change it, but you can move on from it. It's up to you to allow those feelings to go. If you were hurt by someone, prove to them they can't hurt you anymore. Do not let the failure of one person create a huge rift in your life separating you from ever feeling the security of trusting another.

Every relationship you find yourself in will be built upon many things, and trust is going to be at the core. Allowing yourself to trust in another person again will open you up to more positive thinking and feelings that you haven't allowed yourself to embrace. Allowing trust back into your life will help you crack the shell keeping you hidden from the rest of the world. You shouldn't travel through life feeling alone or like you have to constantly keep turning around because you are waiting for someone to stab you in the back. Take charge of your life and your relationships, and believe there are trustworthy people out there; you just happened upon a bad egg.

Having someone break your trust sets you up for negative feelings toward yourself. Were you not good enough, were you too trusting, and why didn't you see it coming? All these questions will play in your mind over and over. The worst part is, there is no answer. The thing here you have to recognize is when someone wrongs you, it's in their hands. They messed up; they did something wrong. You cannot account for their actions. You shouldn't suffer because someone else did something they should not have. These questions will replay for as long as you allow them to because you will never get a good enough answer. You have to just let them go, and accept that it happened. You have to move on.

Think of it like this. You decide to go for a walk on your lunch break, it's a beautiful summer day and you need some fresh air, but as you are walking you get stung by a bee on your cheek. It hurts, it really sucks, and it was super unfortunate. However, you take an Advil, throw an ice pack on it, and you go about your day. Why? Because what else are you doing to do? Are you going to ask yourself over and over why you? Are you going to think about that dumb bee for the rest of your life, wondering why it chose you over everyone else walking the same path? I really hope the answer is no. Please tell me your answer was no. You probably will tell me the answer is no, and why? Because we will never be able to sit down face to face with said bee and ask them why they decided to sting you. You are never going to know why that bee chose to hurt you! You have to keep this in mind for so many negative situations in your life. Are you going to allow this one bee to stop you from taking a walk on your break ever again? No, probably not. So don't let someone who broke your trust in any other situation stop you from taking your walk through life. Forget that darn bee and keep on stepping.

Separation

This is a huge issue, especially for parents. The fear of letting a loved one out of your sight can be overwhelming. Parents are terrified of all the things the world is capable of, and we tend to hold onto our children in order to keep them safe. There is always that fear when someone you love walks out the door they may never come back. The fear of the unknown is a huge trigger for overthinking negative thoughts.

Allowing yourself to go down the rabbit hole of what could or might happen will keep you nervous and anxious the whole time you are separated from whoever it is you are worried about. Whether that be a spouse or child, elderly parent, or a dear friend.

Acknowledging this as an issue is the first step to getting better. Of course, it is human nature to feel anxious about the world around us, but when it interferes with our daily lives it's time to find a way to manage it. Allow your mind to explore the worry and then put it to rest with a reassuring outcome to every situation.

Unknowingly, you are creating a very unhealthy relationship between yourself and whomever you are worried about. There is a good chance that person is going to start to resent you or become extremely irritated about how you react when they leave the house. You may feel this is a form of caring and protection but to the opposite party, they see it as overbearing and untrusting. A child can feel you don't trust they can make the right choices, whereas a spouse can feel you don't trust their intentions. You are putting tension on the very relationship you are trying so hard to protect. No one wants to feel bad about leaving because they know it's going to cause you anxiety. It will become overwhelming for everyone around you. Before you can correct the act, you must first understand why it is you are doing it.

<u>Separation Anxiety</u>: This formerly was considered a condition experienced by children, however more and more adults each year are being diagnosed. This is a medical condition, more specifically a mental disorder. However, physical

symptoms are commonly connected to it. You may feel sick to your stomach, get headaches during the stress period, or even a sore throat. The feeling of stress is literally making you sick. So why are you having such a hard time letting go?

As an adult, there are three major reasons for the onset of separation anxiety. The more obvious being the loss of someone very close to you as a child. The death of a sibling or a parent can make you subconsciously hold on to everyone you love tightly so you won't have to experience that pain ever again. In your mind, knowing where everyone is at all times will reduce the chances of something bad happening to them.

The second reason is that it started in childhood and you never grew out of it. It followed you into adulthood and now you have more ways to hold on to it. As a child, you learn to let go because there is not much you can do to change the outcome; if those feelings are still there as you mature, you will get to a point where you feel you have the power to control your surroundings and everyone within them.

Lastly, something traumatizing happens to you as an adult and you cannot mentally recover. A divorce, losing a home, losing a spouse. This goes back to control. You couldn't control that large situation you were faced with, and it ended so badly that now you want to control everything in your world because it helps you feel like you can stop bad from happening again. I hate to tell you this, but it's not going to work. You can't prevent bad. You can't stop a tragedy, and all you are doing is making a mess out of the good relationships you have now in the present.

"My daughter just went on her first date, what if they get into a car accident?" Yes, that could happen, anything can happen—acknowledge this, and say to yourself, *"My daughter just went on her first date; although they could get into an accident, it's not likely, and I hope she has an amazing time."*

The key is to reassure yourself, and then allow more positive thoughts to take over the negative ones.

Feelings (Love, Hate, Empathy)

Do you find yourself overthinking your feelings? Questioning whether or not you should be feeling that particular way? Do you get mad at yourself because you still love the ex that cheated on you last spring, or because you hate your job and wish you didn't? Are you so empathetic that you get overwhelmed because you can't let go of the feelings surrounding you all day long from other people?

Our feelings and emotions can be exhausting. They can cause us so much more pain than any physical harm ever could. People who tend to overthink things especially have trouble healing from where their emotions take them from day to day. Physical pain can subside and will eventually dull away, emotional pain can be replayed over and over if we let it.

When you have feelings for someone you tend to make their problems yours, you take on their feelings and emotions as well as your own. Whether it's because you care about them or you completely loathe them, thinking nonstop about them has made a large impact on your life.

Learning how to manage your feelings in a healthy way can make all the difference in the world. I am very guilty in this category. When I love, I love wholeheartedly. When I care about something, I care deeply, and when I am angry at someone, you better believe the whole world is going to know. I can be intense, and I can be known to wear my feelings on my sleeve; however, this did become a huge problem in my life, and it will for you as well.

I had an employer who once told me, "You care too much, you put the weight of the world on your shoulders, you just need to relax." This statement was made after months of me trying to come up with ways to help our flawed management, and to make changes in our offices that would help our workers and our patients. Months of me working long hours or giving management researched ideas that I thought very hard about. I worked in a doctor's office! Can you believe it? I cared too much? Cared too much about the people I was there to help, to make feel better, to take care of. I was so frustrated with this statement, I just couldn't understand why he would even say that; after all, he was a DOCTOR. But now I do. I was literally putting so much time and energy into what I felt was right in helping others that I wasn't taking care of myself. This is where "feelings" can get tricky. I allowed my feelings and emotions to consume me. Even though my heart was in the right place, I lost myself trying to take on so much by myself in areas where I had such little say. These actions taken, fueled by my emotions, didn't help anyone and eventually had me mentally and emotionally drained.

Having any type of feelings, good or bad, needs to be reasonable. It's important to care, get angry, or love. It's when these feelings start affecting your mood and actions that you need to take a step back. You can't truly help anyone else until you are okay.

Keeping these feelings in check is important to living a healthy natural existence. I hated my boss, or I thought I did. He was rude, lacked empathy, and didn't show any appreciation to his workers who tried their hardest to make the workplace a better place. I kept getting angry and expressing that anger, and he simply didn't care. I would then go to a place of depression and sadness, and he kept working like I wasn't even there. I tried a new approach and put my everything into being happy and spreading happiness throughout all of our other offices; he didn't blink an eye. I went through a whirlwind of emotions for years. I would cycle through them like they were seasons, and my boss's attitude never changed. To sum it up, I was ruining who I was because of someone else who didn't even care if I existed. Never let your feelings get in the way of your happiness.

Chapter 2: Stop Trying to Impress

We are taught from a very young age that we are put on earth to please others. We must get the approval of our parents, teachers, priests, friends—the list goes on and on. We do our absolute best to make sure everything we do is making others happy whether it's making us happy or not.

It's because of this we start to doubt ourselves and what we feel is important in our lives. We start to second guess ourselves often and we start to doubt our own feelings. This is when we start to *overthink* the way we are doing things and try to mold our thoughts to that of those around us. We stop believing what we are saying and doing is right and twist our thoughts to mimic that of others, so we feel accepted and validated.

Now, it is important to remember that you do share the planet with the entire human species, and being polite and considerate is still important, but you don't have to put your feelings toward the bottom of the list. Remember, you do matter and what you think does mean something.

Stop Trying to Keep Up with Others

No more "keeping up with the Joneses" or these days the soccer moms. You don't have to be like them to fit in. It's often we find ourselves struggling to fit into a conversation we know little about just to be included in the group. We are all guilty of this, it's human nature to want to be included. Most of the time it is not an issue. However, if you start to change your personal views or opinions to get the approval of those around you, that's when you need to worry.

Do not contort who you are to be another face in the crowd. It is okay to stand out, whether or not it's for the same reason as everyone around you. You do not need the approval of anyone as long as you approve of yourself. Now I mean truly approve of yourself. If you are self-medicating with wine or eight months behind on your child support, being okay with it doesn't make it okay. However, if you are in this position, I believe deep down no matter what you say, you do not approve of yourself. But, that's for another book.

There is nothing better than standing out in the crowd because you are accomplished, you are amazing, you are beautiful, or you are unique. Even if that means you are different. Chances are good, if you are holding your head high then the people around you will want to interact with you. And the ones that do will more likely than not have the same views and interests as you as well. When that happens, you don't have to feel like you need to transform who you are to fit in because you will be surrounded by those who love who you are.

If you really find yourself seeking attention from others, then join a club or go into online forums for things that interest you. If you really need to feel like you belong, then go to the places where you feel the most comfortable. Don't change who you are just to fit in, change the location you are looking at to fit with who you are. Have you considered looking into any of the options below?

Online chat rooms	Book clubs
Painting classes	Writing classes
True Crime forums	Yoga or Pilates classes
Bird Watching groups	Hiking groups

What about doing something you love, surrounded by people you fit in with, while also helping others?
Habitat for Humanity
Animal Rescues like ASPCA
Animal Sanctuary
Community food banks
Donate time at nursing homes or hospitals

All these options will not only help you surround yourself with people who share your interests and values, but you will be doing something that helps others. This in turn will make you feel so much better about yourself, allowing you to let go of some of that internal negative talk.

You can't change the way others respond to you or to who you are. Stop overthinking all the reasons you may not fit in with a certain crowd, and start trying to find a crowd that welcomes you with open arms. You will in time find these are the people you want to be surrounded by anyway.

Stop Trying to Impress Your Boss

We like to believe we can do everything. Most overthinkers feel that they hold the key to extending the hours in the day, and can accomplish every task they are given, and then they ask for more. Sadly, this is a hard truth that at some point you must admit to yourself is unobtainable. You can't do it all and then some. If you could, you wouldn't be forced to overthink everything you did day after day hoping you got it right. It's time to accept that you aren't perfect and honestly, no one expects you to be.

Storytime: I spent years trying to impress the higher-ups at the doctor's office I worked for. I would take on jobs that were not in my job description, I would help anyone who asked, and I would even ask for more responsibility. Well, I got it. I would get a "thank you." Or maybe even a "what would we do without you"; at the most a fifty cent raise every year or so. You know what I didn't get? Appreciation or the feeling of self-worth. I always questioned why I was working so hard, and it constantly went unnoticed or unappreciated. I was literally driving myself insane to the point of a literal mental breakdown at least once a year. Twice, TWICE, my doctor took me out of work for a week because of my physical state due to my mental exhaustion.

Why? What was the reason I kept abusing myself for a company that did not care? Because I hated feeling less than. If I wasn't the hardest working person there, doing the best job I could, I felt little in the eyes of management. I let myself overthink the lack of appreciation from my superior. I allowed myself to believe that they weren't appreciative enough because I was not doing enough. I worked harder and harder to get noticed by people who were never going to notice me. In turn, I was keeping myself away from those who did appreciate me and notice me. I was working so hard at the office that I was distant at home. I allowed myself to pull away from my kids and my husband who does love me, who does care about me, and who does need me every single day, in order to give 1,000% of myself to people who thought of me like a dime a dozen.

Why do we do this? Why do we try so hard to get the approval of those who don't care? Have you ever heard the saying, "Ask the busiest person in the room for help?" It's because those are the people you can count on to never say no. That's right, I am calling us Yes-men. All of us. We are all so determined to look needed and helpful that we will say yes to everything. In the end, we lose ourselves and those who mean the most to us.

Are you that person who will say yes even though your brain is screaming NO! so loud you can barely think straight? You don't have it in you to admit you just cannot handle one more thing? Do you always say yes because you are afraid of what opportunity you may end up missing because you said no? Or, are you the person who says yes to everything because you honestly just don't want to disappoint the person who is asking? No matter the reason you keep saying yes, most of the time we are not saying yes because we want to. And when we are saying yes because we feel we need to, it becomes an action we regret, one that we despise, a situation that is going to put us in a bad mood. Unfortunately, these feelings are going to come out on the people who are there for you, the ones who will listen to us and take the brunt of our frustration.

We tend to take for granted the people who truly matter in order to impress those who could care less if you were there or not. Whoever said "Our positions can be replaced at work, but they can never be replaced at home," has got to be one of the most insightful people alive. It could not hold truer. Things at home start to break down when you can't give your family your all. Let me tell you, it is not worth it. It's not fair to your family, and it's not fair to you. Never give someone extra of yourself if they don't earn it, because they simply do not deserve it.

Look back at the time already wasted. How many days have gone by that you weren't happy because of someone else? How many days did you miss out on enjoying the little things only to sit around replaying a situation in your head over and over wondering how you could have done it differently, or thinking about why the way you did it just didn't work? You are only given one life—stop watching it go by without you.

You Don't Need to be Loved by Everyone

No one is liked by everyone. People will not like you, for whatever reason, and that is okay. Do you like everyone you meet? Have you ever walked into a room and felt this negative, unexplainable vibe from someone and you automatically don't want to talk to them? You just didn't click. That's great, that's normal. We were given different personalities for a reason, and sometimes you are just not compatible with someone else. There doesn't have to be an explanation for it, you do not need to understand it. You just need to accept it. Do not put yourself in a position to try and find out why. It's just not going to happen. Also, never push back against those feelings. Be mature and respectful but do not try and make a connection with someone who isn't a right fit for you.

Are you one of those people who will bend over backward for just about anyone because you want them to like you? You may never see that person again for the rest of your life, and that's okay, but they still have to like you, right? If they don't, you will spend your nights lying in bed, repeating the conversations you had with that person over and over again, wondering what YOU did wrong to make them not like you? What could you have said that was offensive? Is it the way you looked at them when they were talking? Did you forget to offer them a drink while they were at your home? This line of thinking is what gets us caught up in the downward spiral of overthinking our entire life.

Not everyone is going to like you, and that is just fine. Can you imagine having a million, trillion friends who want to hang out all the time or text and call your phone 24/7? Can you imagine the news feeds in your social media accounts going haywire because of all the comments you get? It's true that the human species is a social one, but that does not mean we have to be social with everyone we come in contact with. Having too many people to give your attention to can be just as bad as not having enough. You will wear yourself thin, and your feelings will not be as sincere. The quote of the chapter: "Give them your presence, not your presents." Just like you, your family and friends want you, all of you. Not just what you have to give on the outside. You can give your child a thousand dollars to go out shopping with their grandparents while you go out with friends. In ten years, they will remember that amazing day spent on a shopping spree with their grandparents. Not that amazing day they were handed a thousand dollars.

This scenario plays out for all your relationships. Whether it's time spent with your bestie or a handwritten letter mailed to your brother who moved across the state. Giving your time to those who matter the most is more important than handing out a tiny piece of you to hundreds of people. So stop worrying about how your mistakes or actions can affect how people who probably do not care see you.

Okay, so maybe you did come off a little cocky when discussing politics or even worse, going head-to-head about a bogus call during last night's football game. Decide if it's worth your time to correct the situation. Decide if it was even something anyone will remember a week from now. If the argument was two-sided, then you both were at fault. There is no reason to reach out or hurt your head trying to find a way to make it right. If you were extremely out of line, as a decent human being, an apology may be in order, but only if that person means something to you. Nine times out of 10, if it was someone you barely knew or a friend of a friend, they don't care what you said to them and will probably not be replaying the conversation over in their head daily, unless they too are overthinkers.

    The best thing that ever happened to me was the day I realized no one cares. I am not someone people are going to go home and think about. My opinions do not matter to everyone and they probably won't even give me a second thought. When I truly let that sink in and allowed myself to believe it...so much weight was taken off my shoulders you could probably see me physically relax. I don't have to work hard to impress everyone because they don't give a sh**. I can save that extra time on my make-up and keep those jeans in my dresser drawer for a day that I want to impress, that I need to make a good impression. Job interviews, date nights, visiting the in-laws. I am now totally okay going to my son's soccer games in sweatpants and a hoodie. Yikes!

    The thing you really need to take away from this chapter is, if you don't get along with someone who doesn't like you for the person you are when you are comfortable in your own skin, then why would you want to be around them anyway? There are 7.8 billion people living in the world today. (It's true, I looked it up, check out PRB.org.) I promise you, there will be at least a handful out there who share your interests, appreciate who you are, and will want to be around you for you! A few genuine true friends are all you need.

Chapter 3: How Overthinking Can Cause Physical Pain and Illness

When you are overthinking everything you do, or learn to feel inadequate or less than others, you can cause some serious health problems that will take years to overcome. Many of these problems stem from mental illnesses but can lead to some serious physical ones too.

I think it is important to remind everyone that this book is not to point out your flaws and judge you. We are pointing out your flaws to show you where they are leading you if you're not already there, and how it is affecting your daily life. This book is being written because we truly care about each and every one of you reading this. Why? Because if you are reading this book it's because you are seeking out help from anywhere you can find it to make yourself feel better. You are looking for someone who knows what you are going through, someone who has gone through it, and someone who has seen the light at the end of the tunnel.

We truly care about you because you are worth being cared about. Everyone is worth being cared about, and everyone deserves to be loved, to feel love, to have love. Everyone should be happy with whatever life they are given. Life is hard. Wait, that's an understatement. Life is really, really hard. However, we are all going through it together. We are all living on the same planet at the exact same time and to survive we have to all work together. Each of us plays a role on earth during the time we are here. It's time to figure out who you are supposed to be. But until you know who you are, you are going to let the influence of others, and the negative thoughts you put onto yourself, cause nothing but pain. Let's see just what you are doing to yourself without even realizing it.

Anxiety

Have you ever gotten yourself so stressed out you start to tremble, you can't control your breathing, and your chest gets tight? No matter how hard you try, you cannot calm down? More likely than not, you had a panic attack. Although you would swear you were suffering from a heart attack due to the mimicking symptoms, a panic attack is less dangerous but just as scary.

These days more than ever people stress out about many things daily. You worry about an upcoming test, a plane ride, or spilling your hot coffee on that poor guy quietly reading on the bus next to you. These thoughts race through your mind until they completely consume you. So many people allow stress to take over their daily routines and never realize it, until it's too late.

Millions of people are diagnosed each year with anxiety and it keeps getting worse. It's pretty safe to say that stress isn't going anywhere, so to deal with life, you need to be able to control it.

At the beginning of 2020, COVID-19 took over the world, people lost their jobs, lost their loved ones, and lost their sanity. The terrifying thought that anyone could succumb to this widespread virus was haunting.

<u>*Signs and Symptoms of Anxiety*</u>

Heart palpitations
Panic attacks
Irritability
Restlessness
Fatigue
Fear
Excessive worrying
Insomnia
Nausea
Lack of concentration
Racing thoughts

Anxiety can be a sneaky little bugger. Creeping up on you when you didn't even realize you were anxious. It can appear out of nowhere fast and furious, and for those of you who suffer from any type of anxiety disorder, this can ruin an entire day.

I have come in close contact with people who suffer from many types of anxiety disorders. This includes general anxiety, social anxiety, PTSD or Post Traumatic Stress Disorder, etc. They all say the same thing: it takes a hard toll on their quality of life.

A man I know very well has been suffering for over 20 years with PTSD. As a child, he went through so much abuse and neglect it's a miracle he was able to make it through life as far as he did successfully. He was a hard worker and a very caring man who would help anyone at the drop of a hat. When he turned 19 years old his daughter was born, and although on the outside, and in his heart, he loved that little girl and his then-girlfriend (now wife), the birth of their child triggered his build-up of anger and rage from his childhood. He was hard to live with, always yelled, would become overbearing and mean for no reason. When he wasn't in a fit of rage, he was quiet and distant; his wife looks back now and says she could tell when he was in these moments because there was nothing but black in his eyes. He eventually came close to losing it all one day when he snapped and went into a wave of a scary, anger-filled tangent, punching holes in the walls, and name-calling things you should never say to someone you love. His girlfriend had enough and she left. She didn't come back until he acknowledged his problems and got help, and he did.

    That's one of the dozens of stories I can tell you that has happened to the people I know and love. That is the sad truth of how anxiety can ruin so many lives. Just one person who has the disorder can hurt everyone around them, including the ones they love. Do not let anxiety control you. Do not let it take over and become who you are. Get help as soon as you notice it's more than just the average amount of stress. You never know who you are hurting until the fog is gone.

By the way. The man with PTSD is my husband, I was the one who left, and he did get help. We have three beautiful kids now and a home full of dogs, cats, and a whole lot of love. He is my best friend, my rock, and my soulmate. There is no cure for PTSD and he still struggles at times, but he has never gone back to the scary aggressive man I had seen many years ago. His eyes have never gone black since then either.

Insomnia

There is nothing worse than lying in bed replaying something you did over in your mind, ashamed, embarrassed, or even angry about it. It could have been something as innocent as slipping in the cafeteria at lunchtime in front of your colleagues or burping in the line at the bank loud enough for everyone to hear. No matter the reason, if you are an overthinker, you are going to be thinking about this nonstop, including at night when the lights are out and the house is quiet. You are going to try to figure out how you could have let it happen, what you could have done differently, and how can you possibly step foot in the office tomorrow? This is going to make you lose a lot of sleep, which will lead you to insomnia, and that can be dangerous to your health for so many reasons.

Signs and Symptoms of Insomnia

Difficulty sleeping at night
Waking up in the middle of the night
Headaches

Not feeling rested in the morning
Depression
Irritability, depression, or anxiety
Slow reaction time
Lack of concentration

A good night's sleep is very important to your overall health. Sleeping rejuvenates the body and heals muscles and joints. Sleep boosts the immune system and will improve your mood. Sleep is so important we are going to break this down further for you in its very own chapter later in the book.

Depression

Eventually, all this self-doubt and overthinking every second of your life will lead you to become depressed, if you're not already there. If you feel bad about who you are, where you are in life, or the things you do, then you're not going to be able to enjoy your life and the things you have. This type of thinking will make you feel alone. If you have decided that you are not good enough, you're going to believe that's how everyone else feels too.

Depression is a silent disease that affects a large group of people. Some struggle with it daily, but everyone has experienced it at one time or another. Depression will take up your time and waste your days that you could be spending with family and friends, or experiencing something you once enjoyed. When you suffer from depression, you find you are not living, you are just existing.

Signs and Symptoms of Depression

Always worrying
Feeling restless
Fatigue
Feeling worthless
Feeling excessive guilt
Irritability
Becoming reckless
Always feeling sad
Loss of appetite
Feeling alone when you are surrounded by people
Withdrawing from your loved ones

    Depression is a very serious illness and needs to be handled immediately and by a professional. Never let depression last long and recognize the problem when you find you cannot get yourself out of the rut. Depression has been known to lead to substance abuse, self-harm, harm to loved ones, and reckless behavior.

    It's so hard to deal with depression; everyone gets sad. Everyone gets let down, everyone goes through hard times, everyone has days where they would rather get lost in a bucket of ice cream and binge-watch true crime shows in their sweats. That's actually my weekend. Being depressed or sad sometimes is a normal part of life. It is a normal feeling that normal people experience often. It's not normal if it lasts for weeks, it affects your daily life, or it makes you feel you shouldn't exist.

If you are depressed, do not shrug it off, do not be embarrassed to ask for help, and do not let it consume you entirely. There are ways to get through it, and once you do you will notice a whole new and brighter life is there waiting for you with open arms. You are the only one who can achieve this though. No one else can fix you, and unfortunately, there is no such thing as the magic pill. I am not in any way saying anxiety or depression medications do not help people, I am just saying they are not 100% effective. If they were, this world would be a much happier place.

    Learn to respect yourself. When you notice you are falling into a funk, go for a walk or phone a friend. It's going to be hard, but it is important for YOU to act. Think of it as a long workday. Boss was riding you harder than normal, co-workers were driving you insane, then you got home from work only to make dinner that no one would eat. I am sure you all know what I am talking about. Now think about jumping on that elliptical for a half-hour, or throwing on your sneakers and going for a quick jog. I am guessing at this point y'all would rather hear nails scratching at a chalkboard. But, go for the run. Get up, go outside, and run; run in the fresh air, you have a chance to unwind in peace and quiet, you get away from all your stressors, even if it's only for 45 minutes. How would you feel? I'm going to assume this would make anyone feel so much better. Instead of sulking and scarfing down your ice cream set aside for your weekend of true crime, you would have done something good for yourself. That boosts your confidence and it makes you happy. The same thing goes for depression, not to replace professional help for those who need it, but to work side by side. Push through your nasty mood and do something that you will enjoy, something that you will thank yourself for in the end. Medication can only go so far on its own. It may feel like an uphill battle, but once you make it to the top you can stare down at all those negative feelings that are now beneath you and you will feel more amazing and prouder than you have ever felt before.

Fatigue

Not sleeping for nights on end will take a toll on your body after only a few days. Your body is going to start to ache and you're going to start feeling like you're running on autopilot. Everything is going to seem like endless tasks that you are not strong enough to complete anymore. Fatigue can affect your body and mind in so many ways and it can be hard to get out of a negative mindset when you feel terrible all the time.

Fatigue can feel like you're walking through a fog, or like each step you take feels like you're trudging through heavy snow, fighting to get ahead. Anyone who suffers from fatigue will go through the motions of the day without feeling the excitement or emotions of it.

<u>*Signs and Symptoms of Fatigue*</u>

Chronic sleepiness
Headaches/migraines

Dizziness
Soreness
Achy muscles
Slow reaction time
Impaired judgment
Irritability
Slow reflexes

A lot of people have compared the symptoms of fatigue to the symptoms of being influenced by drugs or alcohol. Your mind doesn't feel like it's in 100% control of your body and you can lose touch with reality.

Muscle Pain

Anxiety, lack of sleep, fatigue; all these things will start to take a toll on your physical self. When you are anxious and on edge all the time, you are tensed up constantly, and your muscles are being aggravated and inflamed. You will start to notice that you're feeling sore all over. You may notice back pain or pain in your joints. This is because your body can only handle so much stress.

Many adults that are overstressed will complain of muscle aches in their back and neck. That's because this is the area of the body that stores most of the tension from stress and anxiety. When you are stressed out your whole body will tense up and your posture will shift. You're going to slouch and lean, making your body settle in unnatural ways.

There is also the chance that the muscle pain you are experiencing may not even really be there. This is how powerful your mind can really be. You can make yourself so anxious, nervous, and stressed out that your body will create a physical reaction letting you know something is wrong. Unfortunately, many people who get to this point aren't willing to accept it as something other than just pain. This is when people treat the symptoms and not the problem.

No matter how many pain killers you take throughout the day, the problem is not going to go away until the underlying cause is dealt with.

Migraines

Another condition that can be triggered by overthinking, anxiety, and lack of self-worth is migraines. These can be excruciatingly painful and can impact your whole life. You will start to miss out on the things that mean the most to you, or even days at work. You can get fired from your job or take time away from the people who truly care about you.

When you find yourself struggling with migraines due to stress, they are often recurring. That means multiple days a month you may be lying in bed missing out on the world around you. You tend to sleep a lot more to deal with the pain and you will be depressed, agitated, and mean because you cannot find relief.

Millions of people suffer from migraines every year, and many of them can be the cause of unhealthy stress and lack of stress management. Once you figure out how to reduce the overthinking and anxiety, you may start to notice the frequency of your migraines start to reduce dramatically.

Signs and Symptoms of Migraines

Blurry/distorted vision
Congestion
Sensitivity to light and sound
Nausea
Irritability
Dizziness or lightheadedness
Scalp and head tenderness
Seeing flashes of light

As you can see, migraines are more than just a headache and they can truly affect your quality of life. The good news is, if overthinking is the cause of your migraines, they will stop once you get your thoughts under control.

I am a migraine sufferer. Not the kind of person who gets one once and while and it is awful for a few days, then it's gone and it's another six months before you have to worry about it again. Nope, I get one to two migraines per week. I have had CT scans, MRIs, blood work, eye doctor appointments, ENT appointments, and neurologists have injected medication into my scalp with two needles. Nothing helped. The pain wasn't going away until it was good and ready to go on its own. No one knew why, and all serious issues were ruled out so I just had to cope. Ironically enough, once I left my job (you know, the one with the rude, heartless boss) my migraines subsided. I still get them, probably more so than those who don't suffer from chronic migraines, but I do not get them nearly as often; and when I do, the pain is so much more tolerable.

The body works in some very weird ways when it is under too much stress. The thing to remember is your body is not out to trick you. If you have pain anywhere, it's because there is something wrong. If you can't track down a physical source, it's time to start looking at the mental ones.

Chapter 4: 5 Reasons You May Be Overthinking Things

1. Self-doubt

Thinking your best isn't THE best will make you overthink every situation you are in. Do you tend to think you're doing it wrong all the time, that your spouse is a better parent, your mom is a better cook, your co-worker is more organized? You can't do anything right and the only way to get through your day is by asking others for their opinions or advice? This will get you nowhere. This is negative self-talk, and you are never going to get past the burden of overthinking if you can't trust yourself with making the right decisions.

Each of us comes into the world as a clean slate. We know nothing but how to cry and how to eat. Everything else is taught to us. As humans we have learned to catch on fast and make quick decisions based on problem solving. Sometimes the way to problem solve is through trial and error. You can't get better at something if you don't make a mistake first. This is how we grow, this is how we get better, and this is how we mature. Do not let your faults become who you are; notice them, accept them, and if they really bother you that much learn how to fix them. You cannot let yourself believe that you cannot accomplish something because you are not good at it at the moment. You have to understand that you are perfect just the way you are, and you can accomplish anything you set your mind to.

Let me tell you a little secret: I have NEVER not once doubted myself. There has never been a single task that came before me that I didn't believe I could handle. I knew when I was 18 years old, I was going to turn my life around and be the best mom I could be. I knew even though we had no money to start a family with, it was going to be okay. I wasn't even worried, when we had two kids and expecting a third at age 23, to buy our first house living on one paycheck. And quite literally paycheck to paycheck. And through all of our struggles and all of our hard times we never failed, we never let our troubles get in the way of our success. Oh boy was it hard. I can't even begin to tell you some of the things we went through, but damn it, I was not going to ever give up. I was never going to let anyone see me fall.

This my friends, is a good example of self-confidence, self-love, and self-worth. I may struggle with overthinking, and I definitely deal with anxiety, but the best thing I have ever been gifted with from my father is my stubbornness. The refusal of giving in or giving up. He taught me from a very young age not to quit and to do the very best you can. That doesn't mean do it perfectly, or even at times the right way but just get it done.

I am not telling you all this to rub it in your face, or boast about myself or my life. To be quite honest, I don't wish the hard times we had on anyone. I'm telling you this to let you know even people like us, who shuffle from day to day, worrying about if we look good enough in others' eyes, can still be successful. We have what it takes to come out on top. I am good enough, I am strong enough, my journey is to get to a point where I don't have to worry about whether or not people notice. Me being able to look in the mirror and hold my head up high, proud of what I have been through, and still came out successful in the end is all I should ever be concerned with.

If you tell yourself you cannot do it, who is going to be able to convince you otherwise? You have to support yourself, believe in yourself, be a strong accomplished human being; we can all do it.

2. Low self-esteem

Not believing you are good enough will lead you to feel like you are failing at everything. If you don't believe in yourself why would others? You need to ask yourself this every time you start to overthink anything you have done in the past. If you are constantly looking back on the things you have done to try and find the mistakes you may or may not have made, you will never get the respect and trust you deserve from others. If you are constantly doubting yourself, then you make the people around you believe that you really do not know what you are doing, even if your work is the absolute best.

Low self-esteem could be a problem created in your mind about who you are and what you have accomplished. Or it can be the negative comments others around you have put into your head so many times you end up believing it. The thing about self-esteem is it's yours and yours alone (hence "Self"). You can let what others say pull you down, or you can take it at face value. Be strong, and assertive.

When you look in the mirror what do you see? Do you see baggy eyes, big hips (this is for our mamas out there), and a bubble butt? Or do you see the eyes of a hardworking and dedicated person, child-bearing hips that created an entire human being, and a music video worthy apple bottom? This is the difference between high and low self-esteem. It doesn't matter what others think about you, it's how you feel about yourself and the person you see looking back at you in your reflection.

> ***Pull out those pens again**- Your task now is to look in the mirror, a full body view. Spin around a few times and really take yourself in. Do this naked, in private, without anyone else around to make any type of comment good or bad. This is time for you to start loving yourself. To start giving your body and your appearance some credit for all it has been through.

Now create your lists. Title them, "good" and "need to work on." DO NOT I repeat DO NOT write the word bad. Looking at that word will make you feel that feeling. The word bad will not help you in any way. It will only make you feel terrible, like it's a flaw that changes who you are. Write the words "*need to work on"* because this will be encouraging, this is your list of to-dos. Instead of staring at a list of your negative feelings toward yourself, you will see a list of areas you want to perfect. It doesn't matter what you write on that paper as long as it is 100% truth, the whole truth, nothing but the truth!!! It has to be *your* truth.

Now you have two more parts to this assignment. I want you to take the list of things you like and put them on sticky notes. Place them around your desk, on your refrigerator, in your car, or anywhere you want that will help you remind yourself just how much you love yourself each day.

Here is where this task can get kind of tricky. You need to take the "need to work on" list and separate these even further. One side for things that you cannot change and the other side for the things you can and want to. Remember, if you are okay with that apple bottom you flaunt it. If J-Lo and Beyonce can pull it off, so can you.

With the list that you can change, create a plan of action. If you have noticed you gained a few pounds while being on lockdown during the pandemic, create a healthier lifestyle plan. Eat smaller portions at every meal and take a walk on your lunch break. If you don't like how your quarantine hair suits you, treat yourself to a spa day and get a new cut and color. There is nothing like a little self-pampering to make you feel like a million dollars. Make sure you are setting your goals in a way you will enjoy them, not loathe them. If you decide you're going to break up with carbs and run five miles every day, not only are you setting yourself up for failure and the goals will not be accomplished, but you are going to put yourself back into an even worse position from where you started because now you are going to be upset with yourself. Create obtainable goals and forgive yourself when you slip up once in a while.

Now take that list of things you cannot change (at least without some type of dangerous, unnecessary surgery) and find a reason to love it. Your "flaws" aren't flaws at all but your unique version of perfection. Your body and your appearance tell a story about you and your life- who you are and where you have been. The people who make negative comments on your appearance obviously do not know your story, and that is because they are not people you want to share your story with.

My mirror? My eyes always show my age and are even darker and baggier than most 30-somethings I know. My size 10 frame will probably never display even a size 7 ever again. My naturally long beautiful blonde hair is now glitzy with grey streaks that can only be hidden with an expensive visit to the salon. I have scars, bruises, and cuts almost everywhere you look. My most embarrassing feature, my teeth, are far from being a pearly white.

My story? I have been a mother since I was 18 years old. My goal from that moment on was to be the very best mom and wife I could be. My eyes are dark because I raised three babies while getting my bachelor's degree from home as my husband worked long hours. I didn't ask for anyone's help, never got a sitter, never stopped pushing forward. Then they got older and I kept pushing, working hard at my career and my education, leaving little time for sleep or self-care. The self-care part is on my to-do list.

My size 10 frame delivered three children naturally without any pain medication, it helped purchase a broken-down house and turn it into our beautiful home where we celebrate almost weekly for some occasion or another with family and a large meal. It has gotten me through so many difficult days because it has been strong and powerful. My size 10 body has carried a kid on my back with one on my hip and pushing another one in a stroller. It has carried my sick elderly dog on walks when she couldn't make it back home. This body has been put through so much physically and yet it still stands here today, strong and able. I may not be happy with the condition my body is in right now with size, but I don't want to change it because I think it's ugly or disgusting, I want to change it because it deserves to be healthy and strong. I have truly found a love for my body, all one hundred and *&^^&* of it. Sorry, a lady never reveals her true weight.

My hair has been my outlet every time I felt like I needed to change who I was. I dyed it, put highlights in it, dyed it back, bleached it, straightened it, and as a kid it was permed oh so many times. It was even cut into a bowl cut when I was in 7th grade which was the worst time of my life. When nothing in my life was easy to change, I could count on my hair to give me an easy out and do something quick to boost my moods. It is starting to give off its own beautiful white highlights and that's okay, because it shows my maturity and my hard work. As I get older, and the whiter it goes, the more I'm going to love the look and embrace it. My grandma was pure white, and I can't wait to see her face every time I look in the mirror.

I have a scar on my left finger from a rotary tool while I was making a wooden train set to go around my Christmas tree; a scar on my foot from stepping on a sharp rock carrying my child on my back through a waterfall on a hiking trail we loved to visit frequently. A crooked finger from breaking it multiple times playing basketball, soccer, and baseball with my kids or my siblings. I have so many cuts and bruises from DIY home improvements, taking care of and loving 4 cats, 3 dogs, and 3 kids (at the current moment) every single day. That doesn't mean just feeding them and keeping them alive. I spend time with them all, I take care of them, we play, we walk, we hike, and we make memories. My scars, bruises, and scratches show how passionate I am for animals, how hard working and creative I can be around the home, and how much I am willing to put in, in order to do everything I can for my children and husband.

I will wear my weight, my dark puffy eyes, and my scars with pride, and everyone who knows me and knows my story would never put me down for my "need to work on" list.

Now you take that list and write your own story. Be proud of your body, your appearance, and everything your life has put you through. You should be proud; all of you should be holding your head high and smiling. You are still here, you are trying to get help, and you love yourself and the people around you enough to try and fix your self-esteem to make your life the best life it can be.

3. Past traumatic issues and the fear of them reoccurring

You've been burnt before and are afraid it will happen again. Now it's time to think back. Dig really deep into your soul. Can the source of all your overthinking be due to something that gave you a negative feeling in the past? Did you mess something up really bad in a previous relationship by accident and now you are terrified it may happen again? Looking deep into the things that have happened to you previously may lead you to understanding why you are overthinking everything so much now.

    If you have dealt with something painful in the past, there is a good chance you are keeping yourself in a safety bubble that is keeping others out and you may not even realize it. Instinctively we stay away from what we preserve as harmful or dangerous. If you touch a hot stove when you are a toddler, chances are good you will never touch a hot stove again. Same can go for mental pain when you don't take action to separate the pain from the situation, and the actual issues.

You didn't get burnt because you were near a stove, you got burnt because you touched the hot part of the stove. You didn't experience pain from a bad breakup because relationships suck. You got hurt because you picked the wrong person to spend your time with. If you got fired from a job it wasn't because working is terrible or all bosses are the worst, it was because that job wasn't right for you or the environment was toxic. Move on from these losses and grow from them.

You live, you learn, you get hurt, you don't go back. If you would never touch the hot burner again, why would you go back to a relationship that was dangerous, or a career that just didn't fit? Learn from these hard times to be a better version of yourself. Look at these experiences like rings on a tree. Each one of them will leave a mark, but they also help you grow. You will need these experiences in order to keep gowning, and learning, and improving. Don't look at your past trauma as painful, but as a learning curve, an event that helped you grow and made you stronger.

4. Poor existing relationships

Do you have a negative person in your life talking down to you? Is there someone who can never acknowledge your accomplishments or your strong suits? If you have someone who can never be happy for you or proud of you, then you will never know how much you are worth. This is not going to change until the situation changes.

Have you ever heard the term misery loves company? It's a popular saying because it is true. People who are insecure with themselves and their own lives cannot find a way to be happy for others. This is hard to see when you are the target of their insecurities. You are stuck in this rut of trying to figure out what you are doing or saying wrong, and you haven't noticed that it's not you at all. You will never change the way these people act or think because they are the only ones who can do it. They will never be happy with you until they are happy with themselves.

You have to learn to let go. It can be very hard to do, especially if they are someone close to you, a longtime friend, a cousin, a boss. No one is saying it's going to be easy; you will feel bad, hurt, angry with yourself. Do not let these feelings eat away at you. Remind yourself that you are bettering you, and if that means putting your feelings above another's, so be it. It's not a healthy relationship for you or that person to be in. And honestly there is a good chance they couldn't care less anyway.

There are a few ways to do this depending on who the person or people are. If your mom is judging your every decision, or trying to make important choices for you, whether you asked her to or not, you can't simply delete her number from your phone and never speak with her again. However, if it is a Facebook friend you met in a dog lovers' group, or someone you met at a paint night class a few months ago, then breaking ties before things get worse is the best route to take.

Family

When the one hurting you is a family member you have to approach the subject with caution. Chances are good they do not realize what they are doing or saying is hurting you and they may feel attacked, they may go on the defensive, and they might try to make you feel wrong. Do not allow this to happen. Take control of the conversation and make sure they hear exactly what it is you are trying to say. You matter too!

- **Be strong**- Feelings are going to be hurt, tension is going to be high, and you are going to want to back down. You have for so many years, it's only natural to choose the easy way out. Nothing will change if you back down.
- **Finish the conversation**- Do not start the conversation and offer up some demands on how you want things to change, only to back down after a few arguments or a shed tear. Not only are you going to fall back into the same old patterns, but now it's going to be even more uncomfortable because the conversation was started, and some of your opinions were stated, but never resolved.
- **Do not feel bad-** Yes, you are going to hurt feelings. That's okay; think about how long your feelings have been hurt up to this point. This will heal in time, but you have to get your point across, and you have to address each and every one of them.

Friends

Maybe it's time to start clearing out the old friends list on Facebook, or deleting social media altogether. This anxiety can literally be wiped clean from all of your devices within seconds. Studies show that the rate of anxiety due to social media has increased a tremendous amount in the past decade, and it's no wonder. Every aspect of your life is sprawled out across an internet site for everyone in the world to see. Everyone can look at a simple picture you post and create their own story about you, making up an entire scenario that may or may NOT be true. Just because these people sit in a category on your computer under friends, doesn't mean they are true friends. And if these are the people who are causing any type of stress in your life, or creating stories to make you feel insecure, then you don't need them in your life at all. If they are real friends that you don't want to live without, try working with them.

- **Have a heart to heart-** Tell them how you feel; they may or may not feel the tension as well. Maybe they feel the same way as you do and you don't realize you are being a toxic friend. Be kind but be straight forward, there is no point to a conversation if it doesn't lead to a solution.
- **Take a break-** You love this friend but if they are doing you more harm than good, just step away. If you need time to figure out what it is that is causing the issue, tell them you are going solo for a few weeks to clear

your head. If Disney's Robin Hood has taught me anything, it is that "absence makes the heart grow fonder."
- **Give them an ultimatum-** Let them know what is upsetting you and what you would like to see change, then leave the ball in their court; if they can't adhere to your needs, they don't deserve to be in your life.

Spouse or Partner

This one can hurt, a lot. Relationships between a couple can be so hard to understand. It's the age-old question, "If they were being abused, why did they stay?" Abuse is a strong word. But it's not always physical, however in every form, it is damaging. Sometimes the verbal and mental pain can be harder to bear than the physical hurt. If you are in a relationship with a person who does not support you, or is always making you feel bad about yourself, or even just not giving you the love and attention you deserve, that can be just as hurtful as a fist.

This can be an even harder situation when there are children involved. Trying to make it work for the kids seems to some like the noble thing to do, but in reality, it is teaching your children that it is okay to stay in a toxic relationship. Children who come from abusive homes are very likely to allow the same pattern to repeat when they grow up. Even when your intentions are good, staying in a bad relationship just to keep your family together can be the worst decision you ever make.

Now, what if it isn't a bad or abusive situation? Just a situation where there is a lack of support or teamwork? This type of issue is one that can be fixed if you and your partner are willing to put in the work. If you are in a marriage or relationship with someone and you don't want to end it all, but you feel like their attitude toward you and your choices aren't helpful, you need to have a serious sit-down conversation. It's time to lay out all your cards, and it's time for you to stick up for yourself.

Maybe your partner didn't realize what they were doing was hurting you. Maybe the way they say things are not meant in the way you are taking them. Maybe they didn't know they were doing anything at all. When we do things for so long, they become a habit. Habits, good or bad, can be repeated time after time on autopilot, and we might not even realize we are stuck in them. So if someone you spend a lot of time with has been habitually doing something that makes you upset, but nothing has ever been said, how are they supposed to know they are doing something wrong?

Expect a fight. You can also expect denial and excuses. Again, no one wants to admit when they are doing something wrong. Don't back down, it will only get worse if you can't come up with a solution that works for you both. Who knows? Maybe your partner feels the same way about you. Maybe there is a lack of communication and support coming from both sides. Or maybe it's time to go separate ways. It's better to end things on mutual terms rather than have it come down to a nasty battle.

5. Worrying something terrible will happen if you make a mistake

Maybe you worry that if you mess up, something really bad is going to happen in the future. If you are worried that something you are doing is going to result in larger problems, then you are going to start overthinking every decision you make. It's time to realize that wearing a shirt with a tiny stain in the middle to a conference isn't going to get you fired, being terrified of getting on a plane will keep you from seeing the world, and never trying something new because you are afraid you will mess up could keep you from achieving something you could only dream about.

Never think that a small decision you make is going to change your life forever. Even a large mistake can be rectified in time. There is nothing that you can do that should haunt you for the rest of your life. There is no mistake you can make that will not help you learn and grow in the end.

You cannot worry about things you cannot control. You should never hold yourself back from endless possibilities because there is a chance that something might go wrong, because there is also a chance that it can go right, and it can be the best decision you have ever made.

I have wanted to write my whole life. As a kid I would write poems and even dabbled in some rap. As a teen I created bigger and better poems and wrote my first short story. It was about a heart broken 16-year-old and how she felt about the breakup with her "first love." My future self now realizes it was a horrible and semi-mentally abusive relationship. But that's a different story. I submitted that one to Chicken Soup for the Teenage Soul, but never heard back. Once I became a mother, I went to college to get a career that was going to give me a guaranteed job in the healthcare field, not because that's what I wanted to do, but that was what I believed at the time was the right thing to do. I mean, the chances of me writing anything that would ever get published was silly. I still wrote short stories, or at least started them, about my life, my kids, my wonderful husband and family, my dogs, just about anything and everything I have ever gone through, but never did anything with them. I was scared. I was terrified of being rejected or turned away. I felt stupid thinking anyone cared about what I was writing or what I went through. I didn't want to take a chance on myself and feel like I failed my family.

When Covid-19 hit, I had my opportunity to start putting myself out there. I started freelance writing for blogs, then magazines, then moved up to short stories and articles. This book is my first chance at showing the world what I have to offer, and I am okay with putting that out there to the world. Why? Because I got this far, I love to do it, and even if this book doesn't hit home or help everyone, I hope that one sentence I write down can give someone a little hope, a feeling of importance, or even just give them comfort that they are not alone. I am taking a chance on myself and I'm doing the damn thing. I have finally found the strength to tell not only myself but everyone around me that I fully believe I am worth it. I am important and I deserve to be happy. If writing isn't my true calling and it doesn't work out, at least I know I tried. I know I put one million percent of myself and my work into my writing and I gave it a shot. What's the worst that is going to happen? I'm going to keep writing because I love it, but I will find another passion and another dream to follow for a career. "If at first you don't succeed, try, try again."

Chapter 5: 10 Ways to Keep Yourself in Check

1. Understanding overthinking

There is a difference between worrying at times or getting nervous about an upcoming event, and being a chronic overthinker. It's normal for everyone to allow a big event to weigh heavily on their minds the night before, or to replay a significant life incident in your mind for clarification and/or satisfaction. It becomes an issue when this happens daily or multiple times a day, when you start to let second guessing your every move enter your everyday life.

When you have to replay a conversation over in your head so many times it hurts because you want to make sure you didn't say anything embarrassing or inappropriate, you know you are on a bad path to obsession.

If you find yourself thinking about all the ways a decision can backfire on you and you end up not going through with plans because of what might happen, you are overthinking.

Understanding when you are taking it too far can help you know when to ease up. If you don't realize you are doing it, it will be hard to control.

2. Understand the reasons you tend to overthink

Once you know you are doing it, then you have to figure out why. You may be worrying about things you didn't even know bothered you. Our mind is a powerful tool and can be working behind the scenes. Subconsciously something a friend said to you could be on auto repeat for days and you don't even understand at the time why. Maybe deep down your insecurities are focusing on the words that were said, but not the way in which they said them.

3. Practice mindfulness techniques

Self-help and mindfulness exercises have become fairly popular recently. There are many mindfulness apps you can download to your phone, computer, or tablets. These teach you how to bring yourself into the present moment.

It is so important for everyone to take time to center themselves. Whether it's a few minutes first thing in the morning, or a 20-minute break throughout your day. Being able to take a moment to reflect on all aspects of life in the now can be a huge game changer in how you go about handling any issues that arise. Allow yourself to feel every single feeling that comes through and embrace it. No matter what your feelings are, positive or negative, accept them. Feel them, tell yourself it is okay for having them. And then try to understand them.

Understanding exactly what mindfulness is and how to practice it daily will help you stop overthinking and allow positivity to shine through.

Feel your emotions: Understand your emotions, accept them, feel them. No matter what emotion you are experiencing, allow your body and mind to go through the whole emotion.

Focus on your breath: Inhale and exhale deeply, feeling your chest rise and your lungs fill with air. Now exhale and experience the wind rush out your nose and the feeling of your body's release.

Focus on the moment: Pick one specific moment, object, or feeling and focus on it completely. Understand the feelings and emotions that come with that specific moment.

Imagine a state of total peace: Close your eyes and imagine what total peace feels like. Consider what it looks like, smells like, tastes like. Immerse yourself in inner total peacefulness.

Relax every part of your body: With your eyes still closed, focus on every single part of your body, and consciously allow yourself to relax. Start from your eyebrows and mouth. Relax your jaw, then shoulders. Move to your elbows and each finger. Relax your butt muscles and thighs, then your ankles and each toe. Walking yourself through each step allows you to fully relax your entire body, reducing stress.

Ground yourself: There is nothing more therapeutic than connecting with nature and absorbing the energy from the earth. Talk a walk with your shoes off; if it's warm enough, walk on the beach with your toes in the water. Watch nature and observe all the beauty and tranquility it has to offer.

4. Practice meditation

Once you understand what mindfulness is and how to achieve it in the moment, then you can move on to meditation, to help you get further into your deepest emotions and feelings. Meditation will allow you to free your mind of all thoughts, positive and negative. Once you master meditating you will have an escape from negative thinking.

Meditation is used to improve your physical, mental, and emotional health. It relaxes you, reduces stress, and improves sleep.

Reasons for meditation

Aids in emotional health
Promotes positive attitudes
Improves sleep patterns
Helps relieve body aches and pains
Relieves stress
Increases memory function
Relaxes you
Increases your self-awareness

The goal of meditation is to completely rid your mind of all thoughts. Focusing on your breath or an image and trying to come to the conclusion about whatever it is you are overthinking.

How to Meditate:

- **Find a quiet location:** If you are taking the time to get clarity in life, you need the entire world around you to be quiet. You need the chance to empty your mind and allow yourself to focus solely on your breath.
- **Get to the point:** Go into meditation knowing exactly what it is you want to get out of that session. Say out loud what it is you want to accomplish through mediating. Should you quit your job? Are you making the right choice in a health-related situation? Or simply say, "I need to relax."
- **Breathe deeply:** Breathing deep, full breaths will help you stay focused and also rid your body of negative feelings and stress. It also promotes relaxation to your muscles, soothing tension while you enter a state of peace.
- **Focus on your breath:** After you state your issues in the beginning, do not think about them again. During the whole session, whether it is two minutes or twenty, you want to keep your thoughts only on your breath and how your body

is feeling with each breath. Feel the inhale, the exhale, your belly expanding and contracting, etc.

Meditation can be hard. Yes, sitting in the quiet just breathing can be very difficult. Especially for those of us who are already struggling with thinking too much and never letting our problems go. That is why meditation is a great answer for overthinkers in particular. Your mind is going to wander, and you are going to want to allow it. Work hard to pull yourself back to the moment. Stop the thought once you are aware of it, and bring yourself back to focusing on your breath. We all could use some quiet time.

This is a great time to practice breathing techniques. Learning how to control your breath and use your breathing to relax and recharge in the moment will help you solve any situation in the most effective way, without adding a dangerous amount of stress to your psyche. Sometimes, just monitoring your breathing in a moment of frustration can bring you back from a meltdown or possible overreaction.

Breathing techniques to try

Lion's Breath- This may look silly when you are doing it, but there are many people who swear by this technique. Take a deep inhale through your nose and fill your belly with air. Hold the breath, open your mouth wide and stick your tongue out as far as you can. Now constricting your throat muscles, make a growl-like sound and push the breath out from your stomach.

The Lion's breath technique is a well-known breathing exercise, especially in the practice of yoga, to help reduce stress by relieving tension in your face and chest.

4-7-8 Breathing- This a great one to practice if you are in public or at work. It's not nearly as noticeable as the lion's breath so you don't have to worry about sticking your tongue out in front of the world.

To do the 4-7-8 breathing technique, you have to close your mouth and inhale through your nose for a count of four. Hold your breath for seven seconds, then release your breath and exhale out of your mouth for a count of eight. Release all that air, pent up frustration, and stress.

Deep Breathing- This is the easiest and probably the best for a quick regain of control. Focus on your breathing, relax your body, and breathe deeply filling your stomach.

Inhale through your nose with your mouth shut. Keep breathing in until your stomach is full of air. Then with your lips barely separated, exhale through your mouth like you were getting ready to whistle. Release the air until there is nothing left and then repeat.

These three techniques are all ones that I have tried and have been very successful with. There are so many others out there that could work just as well for you. Finding something that works for you and you feel comfortable doing is key. It may take some time to find one you like, but once you do it could be a game changer. If you are looking to meditate at a higher level, and not just breath focused meditation, you can find many books, videos, and apps to help you learn the proper ways to clear your mind and focus your attention to a quiet space.

The Benefits of Grounding

Grounding or to some, earthing, is a technique that has been around for many years. It teaches individuals how to rekindle their relationship with the earth in order to use its natural resources and energy to heal and re-energize. I don't know about you, but personally I love the feeling of walking through the backyard barefooted. Toes free to move about and my feet planted directly into the earth, not all squished and confined in a pair of shoes. I guess, for me, there is something freeing about that feeling. Just feeling as natural as I can on my own little piece of the planet. Although we have come a long way in accepting ourselves and each other no matter body type or size, I highly doubt my neighbors would appreciate me getting much "freer" than that.

Anyways. Because this is a little out there for some people, I want to give you a mini history lesson. Hundreds of years ago, countries actually encouraged their people to sleep and sit directly on the ground, believing that the earth's positive and natural energies would help to heal and cleanse the body. It's not too far-fetched to believe, honestly. I mean, the earth does provide the nutrition and elements needed to sustain life without any man-made creations whatsoever. If natural soils can grow enormous trees, plants, and DIAMONDS.... How can you argue whether or not it has what we need to feel complete?

Coming back to the modern day, there are still doctors and therapists who will encourage their patients to take time weekly or even daily to take off their shoes and walk outside in the dirt and grass, stand there, and feel the energy of the earth come into your body, and relieve all the tension and stress naturally. This technique may not be common medical practice, but it definitely makes sense. Way before machines and processed foods, the earth is what provided us with everything we needed in order to stay alive. The planet provides food, vegetation, water, and means for shelter. These are all the things needed to sustain life, so why wouldn't the earth give off the elements it uses to keep those items maintained to anyone else who is coming in direct contact with it?

It has also been said that practicing grounding can aid in improving your immune system. The electromagnetic field that flows through our planet could possibly boost your immunity if it has enough direct contact with your body, allowing those electromagnetic surges to aid in repairing and regenerating your immune system.

Grounding through water: Have you ever heard of floating tanks, or float therapy? This is where you are placed into a pool full of mineral water and other natural nutrients, and you simply float for about 30 minutes on your back. As you lay there, you allow your body to absorb the minerals from the water while you are completely at peace. This can be a great way to relax your body and soothe your tense muscles. There are a lot of places these days using this technique to help people calm their nerves and build a healthier mind set.

Take this time to feel your body freeing. While you are floating, you are weightless. Use this time to not only feel weight lifted physically but mentally as well. Instead of focusing on any problems in your life, focus on the feeling of the water, the way you float without any effort, the sounds of the water around you. If you get nothing else out of a float session, get a half hour of blissful relaxation.

Salt caves: Another natural way to cleanse the body and help to relieve stress and tension is through Himalayan salt. Salt caves are used to do just this. The majority of "salt caves" you can access will be rooms filled with blocks of Himalayan salts, and the walls will be made of this salt as well.

Once you enter the room you will sit or lay and simply breathe in the air and the salt particles around you. This can be good for physical and mental issues, but is another technique that has skeptics.

Those who truly believe in this type of therapy say that the salt components will battle the acidic buildup of inflamed and achy muscles. It's also believed that the salt being inhaled will help with sinus issues and infections, respiratory infections or complications, and many other aches, pains, and illnesses. It is also noted by many, that after a salt cave session they are able to breathe better and sleep better. Both of these will lead to a better mood and less anxiety.

5. Take time to reflect on life (the good and the bad)

Taking time to reflect once in a while is important to keep yourself focused and not overwhelmed. This is going to require a little more soul-searching than mindfulness techniques and it may be a good idea to grab a pen and journal. Keeping a diary of how you felt and why you felt that way may pinpoint your triggers and the reasons for your overthinking. Like a food diary when you are counting calories, you will start to learn what situations to try to avoid in order to keep yourself from stressing over them.

Reflection time should not be self-judgment time. Never sit alone and tell yourself how you have messed things up or you can't do anything right. That's not what this exercise is for. Reflection time should be a moment for you to look back at the last week, month, or even years and see where you are in life, how you got there, and what you can do to move forward.

This should be a time where you acknowledge where your current life situations are headed and if that is the direction you want to be going. If it's not, decide where you would like to be headed and figure out how to get there. Make a plan of action; make this a positive experience. Get excited! Are you sick of paying rent and feel like at your age you should own a house? Don't get upset and put yourself down because your peers already have their own homes. So what? If you want to purchase a house, find a plan that works and do it. If you are happy in your apartment where your landlord is responsible for repairs and maintenance, I envy you. There is no "one size fits all." Decide what works for you and only you based on how that decision makes you feel. This is where reflection time comes into play.

Decide what you want:

> -Do not make a decision that will frustrate you or take so long to accomplish you give up. If you want to buy a home, set small manageable goals that will be obtainable in steps.
> -Be sure that decision is not just a want but feasible. Setting a goal to own your home in one year may be possible, but depending on where you're starting is it practical? You do not want to set an unrealistic goal and then feel like you failed from the get-go.
> -Make sure your goal is flexible. Okay, you have a down payment stored away for your new home at month ten. Then, obviously, your car breaks down and there goes four months of savings to buy a new one. Let yourself be okay with pushing that goal back a few months until you can save up again.

Make a plan of action:

-Find the resources to help you reach your goals. In this case, locate a real estate agent and start working with a mortgage company.

-Plan out small steps to get you to your goals. Instead of just saving until you hit $10,000 dollars to use as a down payment, plan to save $700-$800 a month so you will hit your goal on time and know what needs to be done to get there.

-Write a list of what is important to you. In a home, location, cost, rooms, yard. Whatever it is. Make sure it is what you want. This is a life changing decision, make sure it will be something that makes you happy.

-Be patient. We are all spoiled these days. We have the ability to obtain instant gratification for nearly every aspect of our lives. However, when making a large life change, you want to take your time and make sure it turns out to be exactly what you wanted. Do not get stuck in a home that you aren't 100% happy with because you couldn't wait for the perfect fit to come along. (*Guilty*)

Go the distance:

Never give up! No matter how hard it may seem, do not quit. All that time, energy, and work you are putting into your dreams and your goals will one day pay off and you will be so proud of yourself for getting there.

No one has ever said they regretted all the hard work they put into something once they hit their goals. Everyone has had a time in their lives they regret not trying or not pushing harder. There are bumps in the road that will slow you down and even backslides that will make you feel like you are starting over, but never give up. Never regret your life's decisions.

Allowing yourself to realize you want more for yourself shouldn't be a time to feel sad or angry about where you already are. It should give you a sense of direction; it's time for you to do something to make yourself happy.

6. Challenge yourself although it may be uncomfortable

This can be very tricky for anyone to do. This step is hard and can make you uncomfortable mentally and physically. However, once you put yourself into a situation that scares you and you make it through, it will help you let go of the negative thought the next time the situation arises.

So, where do you start? Well, what worries you the most? What gets you thinking over and over about the possible outcomes? Is it standing up for yourself, giving your ideas or opinions in a group of people, telling someone no? Whatever it is, you need to challenge yourself to get through it and stand firm the next time you are approached with any of these obstacles.

Let's say for instance you cannot tell someone no. You are that person who can be so busy with paperwork, appointments, meetings, etc., but just can't tell your friend no when she asks you to babysit so she and her husband could enjoy a night out.

Figure out why you are afraid to tell her no. Are you afraid she will get mad at you? Do you enjoy being the go-to person when someone needs help? Why exactly do you feel obligated to say yes, even though you are fully aware you have no time whatsoever to take care of three screaming children under the age of 8?

Now, say no! The next time someone asks you to do something you really don't want to do, for any reason. Just say NO. You can't feel obligated to make others around you happy because you are scared of upsetting them. It's just not your job. What you will find is that your friend probably won't get mad at you, or your co-workers will love your ideas. If they don't? Oh well, they will get over it, and you will get your work done. The world won't come to an end, your brain won't explode, and if your friend stops talking to you over it, you're better off.

7. Learn how to successfully problem solve

Learning problem solving techniques can be a huge game changer in anyone's life. The way you choose how to approach a problem will give you a wide range of results. Learning different problem-solving skills for life will allow you to calmly and assertively handle any task, allowing you to feel confident that you took care of the situation correctly, and nothing you did was wrong.

Tips for problem-solving: Here are 4 helpful tips to get you through many of your struggles when it comes to solving a problem.

Identify the problem

What are you doing that is making yourself feel so down? What makes you not only tell yourself that you are not good enough, but is actually able to make you believe it is true? There may be many scenarios you can think of, but most of the time they can all fall into a single category. Do you have problems with social anxiety? Is it the idea of being in a large crowd of people, comparing yourself to them, seeing them in a better light than you do yourself?

Is it your current living situation that is bringing you down? Do you dislike the way your house is always chaotic, or how everything is always a mess? This was always a huge problem for me. I am a huge clean freak; my mind goes wonky if things are out of order. Even though everyone in my house knew this, no one seemed to do a damn thing to change it. They knew if there was a mess, mom was going to clean it up because she couldn't stand to look at it. Although this drove me absolutely insane, I was actually encouraging the bad habit. I was allowing this to go on because I wanted the house clean, and I didn't feel like fighting with my kids. I would yell, scream, and complain but I didn't do anything to fix the problem because I saw the issue as the kids didn't help. When, in reality, the big-picture issue was that I wasn't making them help. I was making the problem worse because I was not focusing on the true core issue. Why would the kids want to clean if they were not being forced to? I would yell, yes, but there were no consequences for making a mess and not cleaning it up. I would do it, the mess would be gone, and I would feel better. Kids would continue the same pattern because it was easier for them and there was no reason for them to do anything different. I hated to think I was the problem, and it was the way I did things that needed to be changed, but it was true. Identifying the problem and the whole problem is going to be the gateway to fixing your future.

The way others treat you or communicate with you is a common problem that creates the perfect storm for self-doubt. However, if you look deep enough you will start to realize that the problem is not how the person treats you, it's how you let it affect you and how you let it happen. The root to all problems starts with you.

Try a new way of reacting

Once you know where the problem started, then you can start to form a plan on how to fix it. Make a list of solutions to help relieve the tension and stress at hand. If your problem was similar to mine, think of other ways to handle the housework and the kids. Instead of yelling and screaming with no consequences to follow, create a plan. Find one that works for you and that you can stick to. Obviously, the way you are taking care of the situation is not working, so plan it out. Try another way. Look for help from other parents; see what other people are doing that works for them. Then make a list.

<u>Example List:</u>
*Make a chore chart for each family member
*Make a list of household rules
*Have a family meeting weekly
*Assign a task for each person to do every day
*Take away electronics if messes are not picked up
*Set up a weekly prize if everything is completed
*Make it fun, offer a prize to whomever is helpful the most by the end of the week.

    I am sure you can come up with many great ideas based around your problems or situation, just make sure whatever you decide to use is doable for you. If you make a chart and say if daily chores are not completed, they lose their devices, stick to your word and take the devices. If you can't commit for whatever reason, change the rules. Consistency is key.

<u>Decide on the right solution</u>

    Now take that list and evaluate it. Decide what is going to be the most effective and easiest for you to implement and use. Check off the ones that won't work for your current situations or the ones that really don't apply to the situation as a whole, then make your decision.

    When you start to eliminate items from your list (or add) make sure they not only work for you but everyone in the home (situation). Just because this solution fits your needs doesn't mean it will work for everyone. That will only create new and probably more intense problems. The goal is to make everyone happy. You want a peaceful resolution that will make your life easier and less stressful, but also keep the people you love happy as well. Becoming the best you is not about being self-centered and putting your needs ahead of others. It is fixing relationships, resolving conflicts, and repairing problems that surround you and haunt you every single day. Be willing to negotiate and work together. Make it a team project.

Go to work

Now it is time for you to implement your new plan of action. Give it some time to take effect. Change can be hard and will take some time getting used to, so be patient. Once your new plan has had time to become familiar, it will be much easier to follow, and you will notice your life starting to feel more relaxed and less stressful.

If after a few weeks you're not seeing the results you hoped for, try another approach. Nothing is permanent and no solution is a guarantee—make alterations, minor or major changes, add something or take away. Build a plan that works for you.

Remember, we are all human. Just because you don't follow the plan in place at times, or someone else messes up, it doesn't mean it's a bad plan or that it failed. It means a mistake was made and life moves on. Do not back out of your plan in place just because it isn't foolproof. Allow mistakes to happen and be okay with them. Just that little tip will help you deal with so many struggles.

8. Learn to be okay with failure and criticism

Nobody likes to be told when they make a mistake. Criticism can make you feel insecure. However, no one can be perfect. Mistakes happen and if those mistakes are not acknowledged then they will be repeated.

Accepting your flaws does not make you a failure. It allows you to be aware of the areas you need to improve. Taking criticism as a learning tool instead of a put down can help you grow as a person. It will help you identify your weak spots, and you can build and perfect them. If someone calls you by the wrong name every time you see them, but you don't correct them, they will never get your name right. That applies to every area of your life. If you are constantly making mistakes, but no one wants to let you know, then you will continuously mess up. No one wants to do the wrong thing all the time, am I right?

When you make a mistake and aren't told about it or asked to fix it, someone else has to make the correction for you. If you can't handle criticism or corrections, then you are also saying that you are okay with having people clean up after you. Not only is that not fair to the person correcting all of your errors, but you're not being fair to yourself. You are not allowing yourself to grow as a person.

Now, what if the criticism is coming from a negative person? If someone is giving you non-constructive criticism, it is up to you to walk away from it. This is one of the few times you should let it go in one ear and right out the other. Unfortunately, there are people in this world who think they know better than the rest. If the comments they have for you are not helpful in any way, learn to let it go. You decide who has your best interests in mind, you choose what criticism has some credence. If it doesn't, then it does not matter. Learning to brush off the negative and toxic comments will allow you to leave more room for the helpful ones.

9. Speak with someone (therapist, doctors, friends, family)

The ability to talk with someone and hear opinions on the opposite side of the spectrum can be a very helpful, therapeutic thing. When you feel like you are in over your head, it's easy to get lost in a one-sided thought process, not allowing yourself a way out. If you speak with someone else, they can give you a different perspective in your situation, allowing you to see things in a whole other way. This will help you get out of the hole you have dug for yourself and see other paths you can opt for.

Benefits of talking it out:
- See the situation in a whole new light
- Get advice
- Release built up stress
- Connect with someone
- Know you are not alone

Always know that you are not alone. There is always a friend, family member, co-worker, doctor, teacher, help group there for you when you need it. Thanks to technology, the ability to reach out and find someone to turn to is easier than ever. Sometimes the best way to find relief is simply by talking it out.

10. The power of turning a negative into a positive

Having the ability to take a bad situation and get a positive result will serve you well in life. People who can see the positive in any situation will be able to make the best decisions to solve them. If you are able to accept something has gone wrong and that it's time to find a solution to correct it, you will be more likely to feel pride in your decisions in the end.

Instead of moping around for a week because you didn't get the dream job you applied for, put more effort into finding another job. You can get lost in all the reasons you were not chosen for the job. You can overthink all your flaws or waste time trying to figure out what you did wrong, or you can move forward. The truth is, you will never know the real answer as to why you didn't get the job. Even if you asked the employer. Maybe you didn't get it because they hired the boss's son. They can't tell you that, so you may be told you lack experience or qualifications. Now you are going to fall into a state of depression thinking you weren't good enough or smart enough for the job you have been dying to get. When in reality you were a perfect fit. So, instead of letting one negative ruin your life, see it as opening you up for better opportunities (like one where employees are chosen not by who they are related to, but by their education and experience). You will find another opportunity if you don't give up because something soured your mood.

Chapter 6: The Power of Self-Love

Self-love is the biggest factor that contributes to believing in yourself and letting go of negative feelings. There is no love that is more important than self-love. If you cannot love and respect who you are then no one will love or respect you either. It's like the kid who always makes fun of himself in class. Just because he is laughing doesn't mean he thinks it's funny. It means he is insecure, and he wants to point out the flaws he believes he has before anyone else can do it, because it hurts less if you hear it from yourself. You cannot mask your true feelings and if you don't work through them, it will eat away at you. That kid is making fun of himself because he doesn't love everything about himself.

If you love yourself flaws and all, you aren't going to want to cover it up when you are being hurt. You are going to defend yourself and defend everything about you because that's what makes you who you are. If you are 100% happy with yourself, you won't have to worry about negative thoughts running through your mind all day. You will be able to push them to the side and feel confident you are being the best version of you.

Learn to be okay with your flaws.

    Knowing and understanding that everyone has flaws and being okay with your personal flaws can make a huge difference with the way you think about and handle situations in your life. Sorry to say, but you are not perfect. Guess what? That's okay. No one is. Everyone has their own set of fears, flaws, and self-doubt. The trick is to expect them and accept them. Some of these flaws can be worked on, and in time maybe you can change them. Like cooking, or typing with more than one finger. However, there are others that you just can't and that's okay too. You may take longer writing a paper, or struggle to understand math. So what—that's why we have auto-correct and calculators. The best part about technology is we do not have to be perfect. Embrace your flaws whether they be physical, mental, or emotional.

    Have you ever been referred to as clingy in a relationship? As long as it's not crazy clingy, I promise you will find someone who loves your clinginess. Wanting to be with someone who makes you feel good all the time isn't a flaw, it's human nature. Finding the right person who enjoys spending as much time with you as you do with them will happen; don't give up and don't stop being who you are.

    Are you self-conscious of the scar on your face because people have stared and laughed, or simply because you see it as an imperfection? Learn to love it, appreciate it, respect the way it got there, and accept the fact you cannot change it, nor should you want to. Let me tell you, my husband has a scar above his left eye from an accident he was in as a child and I think it is one of his most attractive features. It gives him character; it tells a story.

Do something about it.

Okay, I know this chapter is meant to make you feel good about your flaws and to accept yourself for who you are, but if you are not okay with something to the point of depression and anxiety and you can change it, why wouldn't you? Don't get elective surgery because you feel you would look more attractive with bigger lips. Don't quit the job you love because you don't think it's respected enough, and don't spend tons of money to purchase clothing you won't feel comfortable wearing because you think it will make you look better. That's not what I am saying.

I am telling you that if you are unhappy with something in your life that you look at as a flaw, and you have the ability to change it, then do it. You hate being tired and never finding clothes that fit comfortably because you are overweight? Get healthy for you! Get up and go for that walk, put down the bag of chips and opt for an apple. You are the only one who can do it for you, and you are the only person who should have an effect on the things you want to change.

Understand the importance of being confident.

If you are confident in who you are, you won't feel the need to second guess yourself or overthink your choices.

The importance of being confident is not to be arrogant. We don't want you to feel like you are perfect and it's your way or no way. Being confident means you are okay with yourself just the way you are, flaws and all.

Confidence shows. Wear it with pride. Walk into your meeting knowing you are going to nail it even before it starts. Walk into an interview knowing you have the job before you even meet the interviewer; walk into your gym knowing you are going to crush that 3-mile run before you even start the treadmill. When you go into any situation with confidence, you have much more of a chance of accomplishing your goals. Why? Because you are dedicated, you want it, you want to prove to yourself and to others that you have what it takes. Being confident is being strong; it's believing in yourself and cheering yourself on in every situation you come across.

Loving yourself makes you able to love others and mean it.

Once you can love yourself, you can love others around you. This will lead to trusting others and not overthinking how others perceive you.

When you love yourself, you will shine, and you will radiate your potential for everyone to see. You will give off the sense of power and self-assurance that everyone will react positively to, making you feel better and more confident. When you love yourself, you can change your whole life.

When you are finally able to see yourself in a positive fashion, you will then be able to make positive relationships that are created from a deeper meaning. You will no longer have to change who you are because you know the important people in your life care about you! This leads to acceptance and feeling comfortable in your own skin and every relationship you have. You can open yourself up 100% and let others in. You can love the people around you wholeheartedly once you believe you are worth being loved back.

Chapter 7: Daily Tools to Help Clear Your Mind and Get Rid of Overthinking For Good

1. Create a mantra.

Have you ever taught yourself something by repeating it to yourself over and over? The ingredients to a delicious recipe or the lyrics to a song? Try doing this with a positive phrase. Do it daily, and believe it when you say it. Feel the truth in the words, and let your physical self react to those uplifting phrases.

So instead of replaying negative thoughts all day long, try replacing them with positive self-motivating words. When you wake up in the morning repeat your mantra to yourself over and over. You can do this in the car on your way into the office, or every time you feel yourself going to a dark place mentally.

Your mantra can be anything. Make it your own, make it personal. Allow these words to mean something to you. Let's go back to the example of telling your friend no to babysitting her kids. Using a mantra before that conversation can help you get up the nerve to do it and be okay in the end. Try repeating over and over, "You are strong, you are important, you can do this." This will boost your confidence and you can will yourself to do something that makes you uncomfortable. Use your overthinking for good.

The more you say these words to yourself, the more you are going to believe them, so make sure they are not just uplifting but exactly what you need to hear in that moment. "You will get the job today." "You are a good mom." "You are beautiful." When these words repeat over and over, they are going to stick. Practice saying them in your head, scream them as loud as you can when you are in the car, write them down on sticky notes and place them all over your desk. Do whatever you have to do until these words are etched into your subconscious; finally, believe them as they are being spoken.

<u>*If you need help here are some of the more popular mantras used:*</u>

- "I create my own destiny and I am proud of it"
- "My positivity will lead me in the right direction"
- "I am becoming stronger each day by facing my fears"
- "I choose to have the best day ever today"
- "It's okay to be wrong, I am not afraid to fail"
- "My mind, body, and soul are beautiful"
- "Love is the only miracle there is." - Osho

- "I change my thoughts, I change my world." -Norman Vincent Peale
- "Be the change you wish to see in the world." -Gandhi
- "Every day in every way I'm getting better and better." -Laura Silva
- "Dream big, do big things"
- "You are the only one who can"
- "You are the artist that will create your perfect picture in life"
- "Every beautiful flower starts as a seed"
- "Every year gives you 365 days of opportunities"
- "Wishes only come true when you work for them"

Now that you have a good idea on where to start, use these mantras or create your own to give yourself a great pep talk every single day.

2. Stick to a schedule.

Sticking to a schedule can help you with overthinking because you will know everything is being taken care of in an appropriate amount of time. You won't have to keep thinking about whether or not you completed a task, or if you missed an appointment. You won't feel rushed or unprepared. Making a schedule and sticking to it can help you feel accomplished and successful, boosting your self-confidence.

Another great part of sticking to a schedule is allowing yourself easy access into available time slots; this will make it so you don't overbook yourself, leading to being overworked with tons of unnecessary anxiety.

Having a set schedule written down somewhere, whether it be on a calendar, Excel sheet, or simply on your phone, will also help the "Yes-men" learn to say no without feeling too bad doing it. If someone asks you to do something, having the calendar in front of you and being able to tell them no and have a valid excuse to tell them "you're busy," may make the start of your saying "no" journey just a little bit easier to handle.

There are many useful tools and apps that offer great "to-do" lists, and schedulers that can make your life a million times easier. Many people find color coordinating tasks to topics works for them, while others love the personal assistant built into their phones that can do all the work for them. It doesn't matter what works for you, as long as it actually works. I can't tell you how many times I have tried schedules and family calendars and none of them stuck. I had giant white board calendars that were completely empty and apps that I paid for only half started. I tried a lot of different ways to keep myself organized until I finally found what worked for me. Now I can proudly say I haven't missed an appointment or meeting in almost a year.

3. Exercise can help.

As you have been taught for many years, exercise is just as essential as eating, drinking, breathing, and sleeping to maintain a healthy and happy lifestyle. Not only does it prevent obesity that brings a whole slew of health issues along with it, but exercise is also important for heart health and will lower your risk of a heart attack or stroke. It's good for blood circulation and your immunity. Daily exercise can help you sleep better and reduces your risk of cancer.

Exercising can not only help keep you healthy from head to toe, but it can help improve your overall mood. Exercising will release a hormone that can relieve stress and make you feel calmer and more relaxed. Even just going for walks daily can help keep your stress levels low. It will keep your body relaxed and your mind clear. Exercise is known to help aid in improving depression and anxiety. When you are doing something that is good for you, it makes you feel good all around.

Many people feel that going for a run is a great time for thinking. They use the time to themselves to problem solve and to decide on ways to resolve issues. You can even use time running to just enjoy the silence. Take time to enjoy nature and the sounds of the busy world around you. Notice the beauty in the world that you would have otherwise ignored and passed right by. Giving yourself the time to see all the good in the world will also give you an open door into finding the good in yourself.

I love taking time to run. Taking a piece of the day just for me. I don't have to give any of that time to anyone else. I don't have to answer to anyone or do anything other than focus on my moment and my thoughts. For that short period of time the only person I am responsible for is myself. I can enjoy a podcast mystery, or jam out to some old school music. I can let my emotions get away from me and have a good private cry for no reason at all, or I can have a good private cry for a real reason that I haven't had time to deal with. This gives me the chance to release any feelings I have been holding in for whatever reason, and to let it all out and release the pressure and pain that is associated with it.

4. Learn breathing exercises.

Learning how to control your breathing, especially when you are upset or frustrated, can help calm your mind and relax your entire body. Regulating your breathing when you are in a stressful situation can lower your blood pressure and help to stop yourself from getting too worked up.

<u>Positive results from breath exercises</u>

Regulates your heart rate
Reduces stress
Lowers blood pressure
Helps relieve depression
Helps manage pain
Aids in effective sleep
Reduces muscle tension

(Go back to chapter 4 and refer to breathing techniques.)

5. *Write in a journal.*

Writing in a journal can be just as effective for some people as talking it out with another person. Logging your feelings every night can help you let your emotions flow and release all the negative energy you could have built up over time. Make sure to include the things you have done throughout the day and how they made you feel and why they made you feel that way.

Use the information you keep in your journal to prioritize your thoughts and emotions. Having a journal will also help you understand your fears and help you get an idea of what really upsets you. Logging your daily activities and feelings in a journal is like logging what you eat in a food diary. You want to see how what you are taking in everyday is creating the results you see in yourself.

Another benefit of keeping a personal journal is positive self-talk. Allow yourself to jot down your good qualities, how you loved the way you put your make up on this morning, or how your legs looked in those new jeans you just bought. Throw in how it made you feel when your boss sent out an email to the entire company congratulating you on meeting your goals a week early, or even how excited you were when you got to the front of the line at the coffee shop and were told your coffee was already paid for by the person in front of you. If you write all these positive things down, you are more likely to remember them. That will help you pull it back up when you start to believe the world is a negative place.

Writing in a daily journal can also help aid in better sleep. If you write down your worries and problems in a journal before you go to bed, it helps you get them off your chest, allows you to revisit them in the morning, therefore aiding in a more restful sleep.

6. Get your 8 hours a night

Never underestimate the importance of good sleep. One of the most important things you can do for not only your physical health but also your mental health is to get a good night's sleep every single night. Following a healthy sleep routine will keep your body energized and rejuvenated. Making sure you follow all the healthy sleep habits recommended by sleep experts everywhere will give you the best chances of getting your recommended 8 hours every night. (Refer to chapter 8.)

Sleep apnea is a common issue that tends to go ignored by tons of people every year. Sleep apnea is associated with not only lack of sleep, but insomnia, depression, anxiety, and so much more. A simple quick fix to a good night's sleep could be with the use of a CPAP machine, or a sleep aid. Both of these things can be prescribed to you by a sleep specialist.

Chapter 8: Sleep Toward a Good Life

I cannot emphasize enough to you just how important getting good quality sleep every single night is for your entire wellbeing. Working for a sleep center for more than six years taught me a lot about sleep and the role it plays in your everyday life and overall health.

In chapter 3 we touched on ways not getting enough sleep can affect you mentally and physically but there is so much more to a good night's sleep, and I felt it was so important that it deserved to have its very own chapter.

Sleep is something we all take for granted. We do not give our bodies the credit it deserves for what it does throughout the night. During the night your body is working hard to re-energize, repair, and reset you for a new day. In order for you to be completely renewed, you have to go through a healthy sleep cycle for your mind and body to have the strength it needs to take on a new day. If you miss even one of these stages or you don't complete it, you can feel awful throughout the day and it will affect every single part of your life.

Stage 1: Non-REM (rapid eye movement) happens briefly as you are in between falling asleep and waking, falling asleep and waking.

Stage 2: Non-REM that happens for a length of time, while you are in a light sleep but not yet in a deep sleep. This stage is leading you into the final stage of shutting out the world and sounds around you so your body can start working.

Stage 3: Non-REM deep sleep. This is where the magic starts. In this period of deep sleep your body will start to work on areas like hormones, muscle repair, and growth.

Stage 4: REM sleep (rapid eye movement) happens about 90 minutes after you fall asleep. This stage is important for memory and emotions, and re-energizing your brain and helping it store the knowledge you have been taking in throughout the day.

The first two stages are an important part of the sleep cycle because they are getting you relaxed and ready to get into the revitalizing parts of sleep. It's stages 3 and 4 that make a huge difference on how you feel when you wake up in the morning. The reason I'm going all science class on you is because, if you know the reasons why sleep is so important and not just "sleep is important," the more likely you are going to focus on a better sleep pattern.

If you find yourself waking up at 6am and still feeling groggy and exhausted every morning, but you know you went to bed at 10pm so you are getting your full 8 hours, your problem is probably because your body is not cycling out of the first two cycles long enough. Light sleep is not going to help you feel awake and refreshed. You have to complete your last two cycles for your body to fully help refuel and repair you.

Have you tried every fad diet out there, joined a gym and attended it every other day but the pounds keep adding up and you cannot get to a healthy weight? This can be a direct link to not processing through the 3rd cycle of sleep (also known as your deep sleep cycle). People who are not getting enough deep sleep have a much higher chance of being overweight and struggling to lose that weight. This is because the 3rd stage is what keeps your hormones in balance. If you're not sleeping, you aren't going to be able to regulate your hormones that help you maintain and even lose weight.

Stage 3 is also important for immunity support. If you are getting sick a lot, finding yourself always suffering from colds or catching everything your co-workers bring to the office, orange juice and zinc may not be the help you need. When you are sick your doctor will tell you to get plenty of sleep so your body can use all of its energy to fight off the illness. This is also the case for staying healthy in the first place. Your immune system cannot fight off all the viruses and illness that are entering your body if your body is not being restored throughout the night.

Finally, and most importantly for this book's purpose anyway, stage 3 is a key player in your mood, and a lack of sleep can cause depression and anxiety. When your brain is not able to release the right amount of hormones throughout sleep, your entire body can be affected in many ways. Things like serotonin, norepinephrine, HGH, melatonin, and so on will affect your mood and how you feel from day to day. A lack of serotonin can cause depression.

Feeling depressed and not being able to understand why can lead to worse depression and anxiety. You can go to many doctors, have tons of blood and tests done, and never be able to find the reason behind your depression unless you complete a sleep study.

Now the 4th sleep stage is the most important for memory and cognitive skills. If your body is unable to cycle through the REM stage of sleep completely, or at all, you are going to have a hard time focusing on tasks, remembering information provided to you, or even getting through your daily routine. Missing the 4th stage of sleep can give you the feeling of being tipsy without ever sipping alcohol a day in your life.

Now that you know why sleep is important, here is a guide to help you maintain healthy sleep habits. This list was created by the Virtual Sleep Medicine App, Ognomy, and is used for all their patients, and is given to people who have found themselves unfortunate enough to have been displaced from their homes for any given number of reasons, through their nonprofit sector, RestCue Kit Foundation. These tips and tricks have helped countless people who suffer from insomnia, sleep apnea, lack of sleep due to depression, anxiety, and overthinking, as well as many other sleep related issues keeping them from a good night's rest.

Healthy Sleep Habits (Ognomy.com)

- Regiment your sleep schedule: same time to bed and same time to rise on a regular basis.
- Exercise regularly each day. It is best to finish exercise six hours before bedtime.

- Avoid naps, but check with your physician first (in some sleep disorders, naps are beneficial).
- Take a hot bath to raise your body temperature within two hours before bedtime. A warm drink may help you relax as well as warm you up.
- Do not smoke after 7:00 P.M. or stop smoking entirely if possible.
- Avoid caffeine in the evening and close to bedtime. Try to limit caffeine intake to three cups per day, prior to 10:00 A.M.
- Decrease the use of alcoholic beverages as much as possible. Alcohol can fragment sleep over the second half of the sleep period.
- Avoid eating a full meal or drinking three hours before bedtime. A light bedtime snack may be helpful.
- If you have trouble with regurgitation, be especially careful to avoid heavy foods and spices in the evening. Do not retire too hungry or too full. The head of the bed may need to be raised.
- Keep your room dark, quiet, well ventilated, and at a comfortable temperature throughout the night. Ear plugs and eye shades are OK.
- Reading before lights out may be helpful if it is not occupationally related.

- List problems and one sentence next-step solutions for the following day. Set aside worry time. Forgive yourself and others.
- Learn simple self-hypnosis to use if you wake up at night. Do not try too hard to sleep; instead, concentrate on the pleasant feeling of relaxation.
- Keep the clock face turned away, and do not find out what time it is when you wake up at night.
- Use stress management during the daytime.
- Use the bedroom only for sleep and sex; do not work or do other activities that lead to prolonged arousals.
- If you are not drowsy and are unable to fall asleep within 10 to 15 minutes, leave your bedroom and engage in a quiet activity elsewhere. Do not permit yourself to fall asleep outside the bedroom. Return to bed when, and only when, you are sleepy. Repeat this process as often as necessary throughout the night.

Everyone has struggled with sleep at some point in their lives. It's normal to have an issue for a night or two during an intense time in your life or when you have injured yourself and you can't sleep because of pain. But if you find yourself struggling for days or weeks, or the issue is recurring, it may be time to seek professional help from a sleep specialist. They can let you know if there is a medical condition causing your problems or if you just need to learn some better sleep habits to help you get to bed on time.

Overthinking is one of the leading causes of sleep deprivation. Not finding a solution to shutting down your brain and letting go of your thoughts until the morning can lead to more serious conditions and results. Besides the advice given above, using the breathing techniques or meditation apps previously mentioned can be helpful to giving you a great night of sleep. Listening to a guided meditation will block out the noises around you and help you focus on falling asleep.

I personally have found that sleeping to the sounds of nature is a great way to turn off my wandering mind and just let sleep take over. Listening to the rain fall on a tin roof, or the ocean waves splashing against the shore can soothe you into a calm and quiet state of mind, helping your worries fade and your dreams take over.

Chapter 9: Flip It and Reverse It

Change the way you think and create a new way to approach everything in life. Instead of thinking of something as a problem, think of it as a project. Nope, that isn't broken, it just needs to be fixed. You're overwhelmed, no you are not. You are simply busy and need to find a great way to organize your tasks. Do not go through life feeling like everything is a huge problem and you are the only person on earth who can solve it, but you have no idea how to find the solution. Life is just one giant mystery we are all working to solve together. Have fun with it.

Acknowledge what has already happened; it can't be changed and all you can do is move forward.

Hating yourself and thinking of all the things you would do differently if you could go back in time can't help you. No matter how much you wish you could, there is no way you can change what you have already done. You need to acknowledge the mistakes, recognize the faults, and then learn from them. If you overthink all the things you could have or should have done differently it will do nothing but push you further into a depression. Why? Because there is no end to that self-discussion, there is no resolution. There can't be. However, if you are willing to understand what happened, accept what went wrong, and find ways you can change it next time, you will successfully be able to get past the self-doubt, negative mind set, and constant overthinking.

It has been said by many history teachers throughout the years, that we teach history so we can learn about the past and we will never repeat it. That statement holds true for life in general. Be okay with what happened, but be sure that in the future you change the things that may have caused the mistake.

Realize all you can do is your best and you are not going to be good at everything.

You cannot do it all. No one can do everything. If everyone was able to get through life without asking for help, the need for jobs, communities, and relationships would be obsolete. As humans we all have flaws, we all have strong points, we can all offer something to the world. It is your job to figure out what you have to offer, and accept what you don't.

Once you accept that you can't be good at it all, then you can focus on the things you are good at. Utilize it, perfect it, feel good about it. It's okay to be proud of yourself and to allow yourself to show off your talents to boost your own ego. Hey, you deserve it. Work hard at it and own it. Then tell yourself that as long as you are being the best you, that's all anyone is asking for. Then realize that other people will come to you for help with it too.

Take your strengths and run with them. Are you good at communication? Work in sales, use your charm to sell products, and bring in a fortune with your gift of gab. Are you outspoken or over observant? Work for new or other forms of entertainment, write reviews on celebrity outfits or the recent TikTok hits. Do you prefer coming home and snuggling your dog rather than having to deal with other people every day? Work for a vet, a farm, a shelter, or any other place that will allow you to interact with our furry little friends all day long so you feel comfortable and happy where you are. There are so many things you can do to make yourself happy working with what God has given you. You can take your strengths and you can work them into your interest so that you are not only good at your job, but happy as well.

You will never be happy in life if you are unhappy at work. If you are stuck in your current place of employment, you have got to find a way to make it work with what you have or you will never find a way out of your spiraling negative hole. Then when your chance comes along, take it.

Remember there is no amount of money that is worth your unhappiness. Whether you are bringing in $50,000 a year or $500,000, you have to like what you are doing or that money isn't going to mean anything. Money can only buy happiness for so long; it can bandage the cut, but it will not heal the wounds. There are people who have very little when it comes to the material things in life, but are still the happiest people in the world because they spend their days happy, and are surrounded by people who love and actually enjoy what they do. If you are waking up in the morning dreading the idea of going in to work, it's time to look for another job. Find happiness in life, then you can worry about the finer things.

Be happy with who you are and what you have, be grateful for what you have been blessed with.

When you are able to see the blessings in your life, big and small, you will finally be able to really be at peace with everything else. It could be worse; it can always get worse. Never take anything for granted.

Use this time in your life to really look into your struggles, your successes, and everything in between. Sometimes we focus so much on the negative that the in-your-face positives can become a blurb in the background. If you spend so much time bummed out because you aren't happy with your career, you can't be proud of yourself for getting to that place in your life. Your boss stinks, you are overworked, you are underpaid. Okay, but you have gained experience, made new friends, and met new people, and you have had the opportunity to try something and make your own decision on whether it was something you wanted to keep doing or not.

Let's not forget to just be happy that you have a job. You are working hard and providing for yourself and your family. You are a bad-ass going into an office every day and giving 100% of yourself because you are a good person. You're a strong person. You are giving your children a great example to look up to, a role model. You have the opportunity to show them that you are going to be the best you can be at whatever job you are in, whether you like it or not, until you are able to change it the right way.

This is a lesson I always try to instill in my kids every time I hear, "I don't want to go to school, it's hard." Or "my head hurts," and my favorite, "the teacher is mean." I always respond with, "life is hard, you're not going to get along with anyone, and just get through your day." The world was not created to make everyone happy. It isn't made up of rules and regulations to keep everyone smiling and content. The world has created order and law to make the world work. It's up to each individual to abide by these laws in a way which will make us happy. This goes for every aspect of our lives, from teachers, to employers, to parents, and to kids.

As people, we have all been given a gift to adapt to the world around us. We are able to take what is available to us and find a way to mold it to fit our lives, our daily situations. The resources the earth has provided us has allowed us to start with the absolute basics and build the world we have today. We didn't get here because everyone waited to be handed the perfect timing, wonderful management, the most pleasant teachers. Successful people have improved our way of life in every way possible because they found a way to adapt, to take the good with the bad and work through it.

Maybe you don't plan on making the next best form of communication, or the fastest car on earth, or a cure to a terrible disease. Even if you are the person taking orders from customers at a restaurant or cleaning stores after hours, do this with pride, do the job you have with all you can offer, and do it with a smile. Without you, restaurants would not be able to run smoothly, and store conditions would be embarrassing. You are important; everyone on this planet who contributes to society is important and if you are doing the absolute best you can, it doesn't matter where you are doing it at. Be important, feel important. Wear a smile walking down the street and your day will go ten times better than if you drag your feet through the door and plop down at your desk. Reverse your thought processes, reverse your feelings, be proud of where you are.

Take the opportunities given to you.

Good opportunities can come in many different forms. It can be in the way you perform on the job, the way in which you present yourself, or even in the way you talk to customers as they come in and out of your business. If you are too busy worrying about how you look, how people preserve your work, or who you are as a person, you may be too busy to notice a good opportunity staring you in the face.

People who think negatively about things tend to not be present all the time. You don't act like who you really are, you don't perform how you can, and you don't present yourself in the best light. In these cases, people do not get to know the real you. They don't have the chance to see your potential or your abilities. You are not going to get ahead in the future when you are having such a hard time getting out of the past or letting go of the present.

Take the initiative to change these behaviors now so you have the chance at a great opportunity in the future. Someone is going to notice, and someone will take the time to help you grow if they truly believe you have the potential to make a difference. Your strengths will outweigh your weaknesses if you are willing to showcase your strength to the world.

There have been so many examples of how being positive in even the worst situations has changed the world for someone in the craziest of ways. If you want to feel motivated, pull up your YouTube account and just search through all the videos of random acts of kindness. It will show you how all walks of life, from the highest paid CEO to the unfortunate person suffering from job loss and homelessness, can show the utmost compassion for those around them just because it's what you're supposed to do. In the end, these people tend to see the benefits from just being themselves.

You want to hear my story of opportunity? Oh, you know you do. Just hear me out, maybe it will make you rethink your "bad situation" and then help you realize maybe it is actually just an opportunity in disguise.

I spent six years working very hard, putting in lots of hours on and off the clock. I helped every single person that would come to my desk or called me. I even helped people without being asked to help. Now,

I'm sure by now you are very aware I did not get along well with the manager; he was not personable, empathetic, and the census is still out on whether or not he even had a soul. So you know I was not working hard for him. To be honest, half of my co-workers were lazy, selfish, and those who were literally just showing up for the paycheck, so I wasn't even helping out so much for them. My hard work and heart were with those who did care in the company, and for the patients who needed me to get the medical help they were seeking. I worked my butt off to help the other overworked, amazing employees who would take on so much because they took pride in their work. I went above and beyond my job duties to help the amazing doctors and physicians on staff who did what they were doing because they truly wanted to make a difference in the lives of others. I didn't come home sad, angry, hurt, and just plain burnt out for any other reason than because I cared. I am an empath through and through; I got my compassion from my amazing little Polish firecracker of a grandmother and, like her, I won't give up on helping everyone I can because there are negative people standing in my way. That toxic environment may have taken a toll on my sleep, my self-worth, my reaction to the way I handled criticism and perception of others, but it didn't stop me from caring.

This was evident in my work to those who needed someone that cared. My patients were always happy to see me and grateful for all my help. The co-workers who mattered to me became my little family who I still love to this day, and the doctors who needed my help throughout my time appreciated what I did for them and that's what kept me going.

Here's where opportunity came in from where I was least expecting it. Covid-19 hit and gave my boss the opportunity to fire me. That in turn gave me the opportunity to start writing as a profession and turning something I loved into something I could do on a daily basis. That opportunity is one that I will always be grateful for, but that's not exactly the opportunity I am referring to in this chapter.

Six months after "parting ways" with said doctor's office, I was at our local Catholic Shrine, walking the grounds with my kids and dog and enjoying the Christmas lights they had displayed on the path, when I received a very unexpected e-mail, from an even more unexpected sender. It was the owner and head doctor of the office I had worked for, for so many years. He may have owned the company, but he wasn't involved in any of the management of the company. So, he is not the heartless demon boss I have referenced throughout the book. He was actually someone I had looked up to the entire time I worked for that office. He was one of the few doctors left who still had care and compassion for his practice, his patients, and his employees. He kept himself distant from the "business" side of the business, but he was always a kind face, or kind words in an email, when he would interact with you.

So what could he want from me so many months after his minion ridded the office of me? He offered me the kindest opportunity I could have ever asked for. He had started another practice and wanted me to take over the nonprofit sector of it. He offered me complete and total control over this part of the company; he called it my baby. Even though the end of my employment with the office was a little rocky, (I also got the feisty side of my grandma, and don't forget the stubbornness of my dad) and my exit wasn't pretty, he still saw the good in me.

He reached out to me because he knew how much I wanted to make a difference, how much I wanted to make a change, and how much I cared. He may have also known I don't play well with others when my playmates are mean. Nonetheless he saw my potential because I didn't stop that from showing, no matter what happened in that office setting.

If I would have just sat back, done the bare minimum to get a paycheck every Friday, and go home, I can guarantee you I would never have been given such a great opportunity. If I let my overthinking and negative thoughts about the place I worked in stop me from caring as much as I did, I would have missed out on the greatest opportunity I could have ever hoped for. Being myself, even in my lowest of lows, still shed light onto who I was inside, and it gave me an opening for something bigger, something better, and something I can be proud to say I can do.

My goal in life is to give people the opportunity to see the lights in their lives that may be blocked by the shadows of negative thinking, blocked out by their hard times and the feeling of no way out. I want to give everyone the chance to live the only life they have to the very best it can be. And now I have the chance to do just that, because I choose to keep smiling when it really matters.

Jump with your eyes wide shut.

Another very important lesson I have learned through the last year is to take every chance you can whether you believe you can do it or not. Try something new, do something different. Give yourself a chance to soar, or maybe even flop. But give yourself the chance.

You have no clue what types of things you are capable of if you don't try. You don't know what kind of person you can be if you don't take any risks. Don't think about it...just do it. There is no reason to give yourself the chance to overthink your way out of a new experience. If you want to do something, dive in headfirst. Who cares if you stink at it, so what if you fail, at least you know you tried and you will never sit around wondering "what if." Obviously, I am not asking you to jump from a plane without a skydiving instructor if you have never jumped before. Don't quit your job as a teacher to help build rockets at NASA, and don't try to perform surgery if you're not a surgeon. I mean, get all the information to research an unsolved mystery even though you have no investigation skills whatsoever, start fostering shelter pups even if you don't have enough room in your bed, take an online course studying a new language because it may be useful in future dream vacations. Take a chance on something you really, really want, and you may end up surprising yourself.

Many things I have done in my life, I have only accomplished because I swore I wasn't going to let anyone or anything stop me from what I wanted. Some of them are life changing, like college and careers; some of them not so much, like DIY furniture out of pallets or home repairs with duct tape and cardboard. But let me tell you, everything I ever set my mind to doing, I did it. I was successful, I made it happen. I did it because I needed it done and I wasn't going to fail. I wasn't going to ask someone else to do it for me; I wasn't going to allow myself to be helpless just because at that moment I didn't know how to do it.

This is very important in life; this is what helps people who tend to doubt themselves and their abilities. This means the world to anyone who can't find good in themselves. This is going to help you reverse that self-doubt, negative self-talk, and the need to overthink every decision you make, because for once in your life you are going to be confident in who you truly are, you are going to feel independent, and you are going to know you matter. As long as you matter to yourself and those you truly care about, you will stop allowing what others think bring you down. Because now you know they are wrong. Their opinions don't count if they are incorrect. Show them just how wrong they are, and then stand up for yourself. This will change your whole life and the life you will have in the future.

Chapter 10: The Hard Truths

This is the part of the book that will be the hardest to take in. You are probably going to read this and either want to hate me or yourself. If it helps, go ahead and hate me, I am willing to accept that if it makes you feel better. But please do not hate yourself; if any of this resonates with you and you start to feel bad or upset about it, that's great. Yup, it's great, it's wonderful, it's fantastic. Why? Because it means you not only see it, but it means you care. If you haven't noticed it before but it starts to make sense, that's even better. Now you know where to start improving. Overthinking and negative thoughts are not just something you can turn on and off. You know this, I know this, others around us, though, they may not understand it. There is no way to explain this to them either. Unless you're in it, you won't get it. That doesn't mean they don't care, and it doesn't mean it does not affect them.

There is a chance that this place you are in right now is hurting those you love. It's affecting them just as badly as it is affecting you. It's hard to see when you are so lost in yourself, because you can't see past that wall you have inadvertently put up as a coping mechanism. You can't tell it's there because it follows you everywhere you go, but the people who are trying to get through it know it's there and they run into it every day.

Remember in chapter 2 we talked about feeling like you didn't belong? How, you could be with a group surrounded by people and still feel alone? Then you start to realize it wasn't the people around you pushing you away, it was you keeping yourself from interacting? That applies in all of your personal relationships, too. Maybe you are sitting in the living room on the couch watching television, wrapped up in your work or a book, or anything to keep your mind from wandering to a bad place, and you aren't joining in on the game of Monopoly the kids are playing on the floor. When your spouse walks through the door after a long day's work, do you ask how their day went or do you go straight to everything that has made you upset all day? Do you call a friend just to chat, or do you only reach out when you need a pick me up or help? You may not even be noticing you are doing it, because you are so caught up in this thick dark cloud. I don't want you to feel like I am suggesting you don't care about these people, or that you feel your problems are more important. If that were the case, I would just skip this chapter entirely. If you didn't care, you would not be seeking help. If you didn't care, you wouldn't be overthinking every choice you make. If you didn't care, the people you are hurting the most would have left a long time ago. I am writing this chapter so that you know you are worth more than you think and there are so many people around you who believe in you and just want to share their lives with you. If I call you out, here and now, you may be able to lift the fog and knock down that wall. *Instead of a pen, for this chapter you may want to grab a box of tissues.*

Are you a mother or a father? A sister, brother, son, daughter, niece, nephew? Are you a student, best friend, pet owner, partner? If you said yes to any of these things, then you are hurting someone you truly love and care about a lot. You are creating mental pain and anguish to those people above every time you fall victim to your negative thinking. If you think you are the only one hurting throughout this time, you are mistaken. You are hurting everyone that comes near you. When you are pulling away because you don't feel like you belong, you are distancing yourself from the people who have never wronged you. The ones who you have taken for granted because they have always been there. Sometimes it is hard to see what you have when you are living in the past, or filling your mental space with regret. Look around; is there someone in your life that could be holding out their hand trying to pull you back into their world? Think about how it may make them feel when you are living in so much despair. Think about how badly it may hurt the ones you love seeing you suffer and having no way of helping. If you don't help yourself, you lose. They lose. No one can help you if you don't want to put in the effort.

How do I know so much about this? I have lived within the walls and broke free. I have also been on the other side of the wall with family, friends, and even my husband. Both sides are painful and exhausting, mentally and physically.

When I was struggling with my own self-pity the last year or so working in that difficult job, I let it consume me. It ate me up, spit me out, and then stepped on me. I was so wrapped up in how awful my office made me feel, that I didn't look hard enough at what I had waiting for me when I came home. They were there, they were needing me, and I was mentally unavailable to any of them. Yes, it was hard to deal with me being sad, exhausted, and edgy all the time, but the thing that hurt everyone the most, was me. I was there, but I wasn't with them. My mind was always somewhere else. I would try to shut out the pain by throwing on headphones and getting lost in a podcast while taking on some DIY project or super scrubbing down my home. The kids couldn't talk to me about their day at school, my husband couldn't get my affection, I isolated myself without going into hiding. I justified this by telling myself I deserved the quiet, I deserved to be left alone, I worked so hard all day long I needed time to myself. This may be true. You DO need alone time to stay sane. But, you do not need alone time all the time. You shouldn't have to block out the world for five hours a day until you can lay in bed and pray you can fall asleep. Losing my job was the best thing that ever happened to me and my family. I found who I was again. The toxic relationship was removed from my life, opening my eyes wide enough to see what I was missing out on. I can't begin to tell you what kind of emotional roller-coaster I was on during this whole ordeal. For the first few months of being let go, I felt ashamed, embarrassed, let down, hurt, angry, helpless, underappreciated, and so many other things that left me crying on and off for days. I gave this business so much of myself—how could they do this to me? Then time passed, and I rekindled my love for writing, crafting, creating. I spent time talking and interacting with my kids and getting to know everything about them that I had missed for so long. I felt more relaxed and happier; I started to love my life again. I am who I am; I am an adult who suffers from ADHD and even worse at times, empath. I have to have a project going at all times, and my mind and body need to be moving nonstop from morning until night. I take showers more than baths, because I can't sit in the tub doing nothing long enough to enjoy it, and my husband literally gets mad at me because I can't sit still long enough to watch an entire movie. I am empathic and can feel what others are feeling without even speaking to them. If someone around me is sad, I am sad. If they are mad, I will be furious. If someone is hurt, I know, and I want to help.

My grandmother (the spit fire) was my everything. She gave me the gift of caring and compassion. She taught me to love with everything I have. She taught me family was the most important thing in the world. And while battling lung cancer, she taught me to fight with all your heart, until the very end, and that you choose your destiny. YOU choose when to let go. When she chose to let go, it wasn't because cancer beat her. It was because she was ready to move from this life, and to be with her amazing husband in the next one. She gave up on life because she wanted to, NOT because someone or something told her to. She gave up once she knew her family would be okay with her leaving. Nothing will take her memory away, and over a decade later not a single day goes by that I don't think about her. But she is the one who helped me get through one of the hardest times of my life, because of what she taught me while she was still here. I made it through because I love it! Use your strengths to get yourself through your dark times. It's going to hurt before it's going to heal. Peeling off a scab over and over will leave a scar, but the wound will heal if you leave it be. Leave the past in the past and move toward the future. Replaying all these negative thoughts are only going to make the pain hurt more. It's time to heal the wound.

    I am far from perfect. I still have a long way to go. But I now have the skill to get me to my destination. You know all about what I went through because you are going through it too. So let me tell you what I am going through as I look in from the other side. This is exactly what your loved ones see with your struggles. This here is going to be what really gets you in the feels. This, my friends, is what we are doing to the people who mean the most to us, without even realizing we are having an impact on anyone at all. I want you to read this story and I want you to replace the key players. You are me, the person suffering is your partner, your family, your friend. Hear this story and feel the emotions as if it were happening to you. If you don't fully understand what you could be doing to the people you love, you may never find a reason to help yourself.

I can also tell you a story of being on the receiving end of all that negativity and self-harm. Let me tell you the heavy feeling of helplessness is still hard to swallow. I cannot explain in words the mental and physical pain I feel every time I try to fix the situation, only to fail again and again. Why can't I get through to my partner, my best friend, my whole world. Why can't I make it better? Why am I not enough for him to fight for me? These are the questions I find myself asking day after day. Even after going through this day after day, year after year. It doesn't get any easier when he falls into these ruts. I did not lie before when I said he got help for his PTSD and anxiety, and I did say it's still an ongoing issue. We are still very much in love and extremely happy together. However, in these times when he is struggling with his darkest thoughts and deepest wounds, I still tend to sit helplessly on the sidelines wondering what I can do to make it better. But there is no answer. Deep down I know he is the only person who can truly fix things for himself.

As I have mentioned, I am a doer. Of all things in life, I am a doer. I will go and go and go until my body literally tells me no more and stops, and that's usually when I go to bed. My husband on the other hand is a thinker. He is an overthinker to the extreme. I may overthink in the areas that make me feel sad or lacking, he overthinks everything in life. The kids can't go on roller coasters because they can break down, can't get on a boat because it could sink, started building a tree fort for our son over a year ago and never finished, because he can't make a decision to save his life, and he overthinks every step of the way. I make the decisions in our home. All of them. I decide on dinner, bills, purchasing a new car, how to spend the money, what to get the kids (well everybody) for birthdays and Christmas. We don't go on many vacations or dates because he never wants to leave the house. He has no motivation and little drive. He's a loving husband and father, he's caring, he makes me feel so special, and he's a great provider. This man goes to work every day and busts his butt even in the hard times of his life when I'm sure he would much rather stay home and work through his sadness. During these hard times though, as soon as he gets home from work, the switch goes off. Fog starts to build and the wall goes up. I am on the outside doing while he is sitting on the inside shutting the world out, so he doesn't have to deal with the negative thoughts and the overthinking. He hides in his shell to protect himself from the pain of the world around him, while in turn leaving everything up to me. I know in my heart he doesn't mean to hurt me, but I don't think he truly understands how much I miss him when he is in this rut. How much I take on to make up for his absence, or how the kids feel when he is shutting down on us.

    As an overthinker, his brain is 24/7 trying to find the bad in the world so he doesn't get hurt by it. He stops from doing anything new because he isn't guaranteed it won't end badly. Who can blame him? No one protected him as a child, no one nurtured him or took care of him growing up. Maybe if they had, he wouldn't be as overprotective as he is now. The part that gets to me is his lack of trying. I don't fault him for where he has ended up, but he is also hoping for that magic pill or treatment from the doctor to fix everything for him because facing it himself is just too much.

    Guys, there is no magic pill. There is no doctor on this earth that is going to give you foolproof advice, and there is no powerful other worldly being who is going to do the work for you. You have to be willing to fight for yourself. "A body at rest, stays at rest." Let me remind you, no one is going to do the work for you! No one can change you; you have to be ready to change yourself. There is tons of support and help out there when you need it, to guide you and help you along, but the hard work is yours and yours alone. You have to be willing to recognize there is a problem and then work hard to fix it. It will be hard. It will be very hard, but it will be worth it. I look forward to the day when I see my husband out hunting with his friends again, or excited to go on vacation. I want him to feel better; I want him to love life. It hurts me not having a partner; someone I can count on and rely on. Someone I can talk to and share things with. But it hurts me even more knowing he is suffering mentally and physically every single day, and isn't doing anything to help himself. It's hard, it's so hard fighting, when you have been struggling for so long, but the end game is worth every step you take.

What are you waiting for? You have already let so much time slip by. Maybe your case isn't exactly like mine or my husband's, but if you are constantly overthinking negative thoughts, your life is being negatively impacted every day. You are not living every day to its fullest. You are not experiencing everything this world has to offer you. You are not enjoying those around you who want to be with you. Not just physically be with you, but emotionally and mentally.

Are you really okay with allowing toxic people or situations to come in between you and the only life you have to live? Are you willing to waste the short time you have on this earth, to push those who care about you away, so you can sit by yourself and be sad? Do not let anyone or any situation have that kind of power over you. You are too important to live a life of just existing. Make a difference in this world. Make memories with your family and friends, check off every single item on your 10-page bucket list. Spend every second you have making those you care about, including yourself, feel loved and cherished. Don't be that person who looks back on life and wishes things were different. It's not too late. No matter how old you are right this minute or where you are in your life, you can change things so that you are happy and accomplished when your time is coming to an end. You can be proud to know you did it. You conquered your struggles and survived. You are a survivor. You deserve the same amazing life as everyone around you. You have to believe you are worth it.

As morbid as it may seem, try thinking about the end, and after. Think about how you will be remembered by those who matter. Think about how they are going to feel after you are gone. Are they going to mourn for years because they couldn't help you get through the bad? Will they be sad to know that you didn't live your life to the fullest? Do you want your children to remember you being lost in your own world, and never experiencing life with them? NO…the answer is no. You want them to know that you left this world accomplished. You left the world after enjoying your life and everything you have done and experienced. You want people to say that they are not sad for you because you were never sad for yourself. You did the damn thing; you made your life mean something. You got through one of the toughest times of your life and you owned it. You are a rock star. Act like it. Take the steps now before it is too late. Take the time to really make each minute matter. Do not let anything stand in your way of happiness.

We don't know how long we have on this planet. It's literally the luck of the draw. It's not fair. Even if you do everything right, healthy diet, exercise, go to work every day, volunteer your time, donate where you can, go to church, it's no guarantee. Okay, don't get me wrong, all these things give you a few extra tickets in the drawing and you absolutely should be doing all these things to make your life the best it can be. But unfortunately, it really isn't guaranteeing you will be here tomorrow, or next week, or next year. Why wouldn't you want to live every day making sure you did something great in case you can't do it tomorrow? "Live every moment like it's your last." Because you never know what's right around the corner.

Chapter 11: Therapy Isn't as Scary as It Sounds

Have you ever considered therapy? Although it is no longer the huge taboo topic it used to be, many people are still too embarrassed to step foot near a therapist's office. This makes me so angry. Out of all the things in the world people can be embarrassed about or laughed at for, or even criticized for, is it going to be over seeking help to improve your life? I said no one can do it for you, and there is no magic pill out there, but I never said not to seek help along the way. The truth is, you are going to need help. You are going to need support in order to get through this. Yes, many people have done it on their own, but I can promise you it is much harder than if you had someone in your corner cheering you on.

Sometimes you are going to have to seek help from a professional. If for nothing else than to have the perspective of someone who is on the outside looking in, not someone who is in the middle of the chaos trying to help you find a way out. Although people involved are coming from a place of love, sometimes their own feelings and thoughts can hurt more than they can help. No one knows exactly what you are going through or exactly what you feel every day. They only know how you're making them feel. They only see what is going on, on the outside. Opening up to someone who doesn't know you on a personal level but has the highest level of respect and trust can help you understand things you may never even have known.

Do not dismiss the idea of trying medication. Needing to be on antidepressants or anxiety medication is not something to be ashamed of or afraid of. These are options out there to help aid you to a mental recovery. Maybe you will only need them for a short period of time, something to get you through the first few miles on your road to recovery. Maybe you will end up taking them all your life. Either way, if you find something that works, it's worth it. It may just be that pill that gives you the little extra boost you needed to get your life back on track.

I personally hated the idea of taking any type of medication. It took a really bad migraine or injury for me to even take an over-the-counter pain killer. But when my anxiety started to affect me every day, I knew it was something I had to at least try. My anxiety started the moment I had my first child. I was afraid of death; I wasn't worried about finances or being a mom, I was terrified something bad was going to happen to me, and I was going to have to leave my baby girl. I literally became terrified that I was going to die. Again, it wasn't death that scared me; I didn't want my child to have to grow up without me. I heard about someone who passed away while cleaning her bathtub because of a blood clot. The reasonable side of me knew there were other aspects to this situation and that it had nothing to do with the tub. However, I was terrified to clean out my bathtub to the point I would have anxiety every time

I rinsed it out. This was the same for having heartburn and thinking I was having a heart attack. I would feel a bump anywhere and believe I had cancer. I remember my doctor sending me to a therapist after going in so many times with fatigue and exhaustion. He finally decided that it was due to anxiety. One specific talk I remember having with this therapist was about why I thought something like this could happen to me. She told me something like this was very rare and would be unlikely to happen. I said, "What makes me so special that it won't happen to me?" She asked, "What makes you less special than anyone else that it would?" The statement wasn't what got to me. It was the fact that *both statements were true. I had no control over a freak accident or a one-in-a-million disease.* I couldn't keep living in fear of leaving my child when I had no way to control it. Instead, <u>I changed my behavior</u>. I stopped worrying about what was going to happen or could happen that had nothing to do with my decisions and decided to only worry about that which I could control around me. I took anxiety medication, and I still do to this day, because it helps me get through any struggle that may come. Life is hard, life will always be hard; it's not shameful to have a useful aid in getting through the tough times and keeping you from falling back into the same negative thought patterns and routines.

Chapter 12: What Other People Are Doing

The most important thing for anyone that suffers from overthinking and self-doubt to remember is that you are not alone. There are millions of people who suffer from negative thoughts and the burden of constantly doubting themselves. That is for good reason; sadly, with as much as technology is improving, it is also increasing the ways people can interfere with everyone's life. Some people just love to make you feel like they are better than you or they are in a better situation than you are. In this chapter, we will list the way others have been dealing with overthinking, and our opinion on whether or not these really help.

Just whoosh it away – When I find myself overthinking, I imagine my thoughts like Instagram posts or Tinder profiles. Every time I start to think about something I do not like, I will simply swipe the thought right away, saying, 'Not today.' I will seriously wave my hand in front of my face and say no, like I was swiping it out of my life.

—Jason Ligue, California
(Construction Worker)

Our opinion: This is easier said than done. However, it is a great suggestion, and can be beneficial by connecting a physical reaction with your emotional one. Using physical reactions to these thoughts, though, is a great way to make a better connection between body and mind when you start to overthink. Physically taking your hand and swooshing away your negative thoughts.

Think good things for others in your life – I close my eyes and think about people I love. Anyone who I know that may be struggling at the time. And I will send them my prayers and wish for them to have a great day, that they find peace with their problems, and that they will be safe and happy throughout their hard times. Doing this makes me feel happier and accomplished. Thinking about my family and friends makes me feel connected.
—Taylor, New York (Real Estate Agent)

Our opinion: Visualizing someone you care for and wishing for their happiness will in turn make you feel good. It's like the theory if you smile it will automatically boost your mood. If you wish for someone to be happy and well, it will make you feel better about yourself and give you something more important to focus on.

One Step at a Time – When I find myself overthinking, I breathe deeply, and think to myself, "One step at a time." It helps me stop the racing thoughts of everything I'm thinking about, so that I can put forth all of my energy and focus on one situation at a time.

—Trinity, Georgia (Bank Manager)

Our opinion: Sometimes all you need is self-guidance and some simple self-reassurance. Stopping to put yourself in the moment and reminding yourself that you do not have to get everything done at one time can make a big difference on how you work through your tasks and your thoughts. If you simply remind yourself every time you get overwhelmed that it is okay to take one step at a time, you are more likely to slow down and listen.

Look at it from a new perspective – I like to stop myself from overthinking my problems by trying to look at them from a whole other perspective. Instead of seeing it as my problem, I will turn it into a friend's problem. From there I decide what I would do or say to help a friend out in that particular situation, then I apply it to myself.

—Bridget T., Arizona (School Guidance Counselor)

Our opinion: Although I can follow her reasoning here, as I like to be objective, not a lot of people who suffer from overthinking and anxiety or depression are capable of doing this. It is really hard for anyone who is used to seeing their faults in everything to step outside of their head and look in from another angle. Most people will struggle to see any situation in another light.

With that said, I see this being a great way for others who can accomplish removing themselves from certain situations. Looking back, replace the words you said and the actions you took with another person's image. If you can see someone else recreating the situation you were in, it will give a good perspective on how you should really feel about what had taken place. For example, during a conversation with your co-worker over a company policy change, you and another worker have a different opinion that turns into an argument that gets way out of hand. You go home at night and then question over and over if the stance you took was appropriate or not. If you can place another person in your place and view the argument as an outsider, it can help you get a perspective from someone on neutral ground. Did you think your replacement image was in the wrong still, or do you think that person handled the situation appropriately and it was the co-worker who took it further than they should have?

Imagine a mental Stop Sign – When I start to go down the rabbit hole of any given problem, I like to imagine a giant stop sign pop up right in front of me. A huge bright red sign that is telling me to stop in my tracks, don't go down that hole. I will dismiss the negative thought right on the spot. For the thoughts that do need attention, I store them in my mental file for later, when I have time to tackle each issue one at a time.

—Lance J., Pennsylvania (Music Teacher)

Our opinion: I have to say, I am loving the way so many people are using the example of imagining physical objects. This is so helpful when trying to distract the mind. Talking to yourself is just adding more voices to your already spinning head. Using an image to literally tell you to STOP, can be so useful for some people who get lost in their thoughts. Picturing something like a stop sign physically getting in your way from continuing to replay the same thought over and over will help you jolt yourself from the cycle.

Hold on to your inner peace – When I was younger, I helped my mom go through a big box of my grandfather's old stuff. I happened upon a set of his dog tags from the war. She let me keep one, so I keep it with me at all times. When I am struggling, I will hold this tag in my hand and close my eyes; this helps me recenter and refocus my energy and attention to the present.   —Jonathan R., New York (RPN)

Our opinion: Okay, this is honestly by far my favorite technique. Jonathan has literally found the best way to combine a form of positivity with an object, in order to allow touch to enhance his mood no matter where his mind is leading to. He found something that he can take with him anywhere he is going without being in the way, but still available anytime he starts to let his thoughts get away from him.

Will this really matter in the future? – When I find myself stuck in the same thought over and over, and just can't let it go, I stop and ask myself, "Will this pertain to or even matter in the near future? Is it going to affect my life today, tomorrow, or even next year? If that answer is no, then I know it's my insecurities making me overthink things and it's time to stop the thoughts and push them aside.

—Derrick, Florida (Editor and Copywriter)

Our opinion: Yes, this is true for everyone in every situation. I cannot say it enough that there is no reason to overthink something you cannot control or change. If you are constantly thinking about the slip and fall in front of your date that happened last week, keeping yourself feeling embarrassed over and over, you are wasting your time and holding on to negative feelings for no reason. Why are you upsetting yourself when you can't go back in time and change what happened? It's over, it happened, and everyone has gotten past it. There is no gain to continuing to think about the past.

Feel the emotions – When I feel myself starting to overthink, I go through a pre-planned process. I stop what I am doing, I take a moment to breathe through it, then I will acknowledge what it is I really am feeling. I allow myself a minute to acknowledge these feelings and why the thought keeps replaying, then I will let it go.

—Lindsey W., New York (Preschool Teacher)

Our opinion: Here is another great way to keep yourself in check and hold yourself accountable for holding on to negative recurring thoughts, when in reality you should just be letting it go. Walking yourself through these emotions step by step and giving yourself a way to feel the emotions and get through them can be a very effective way of letting yourself finally put the issue to rest so you are able to successfully get past it.

This leads back to the beginning of the book, in chapter 1 when I recommended carrying a notebook around with you to jot down what is making you upset, or when you start to self-doubt and replay negative scenarios in your head. Write down the issues you are suffering over, physically look at the words on the page, and allow yourself to feel how those words make you feel. Then allow yourself to feel the release of tension when letting them go.

Imaginary Vacation – When I notice my mind is spinning with negative thoughts, I allow myself to do a bit of daydreaming. I take a moment to escape to my happy place. It could be a beach, a beautiful park, an exotic Island. I just close my eyes and boom, I am there. It makes me feel happy and calm in the moment. When I open my eyes, I feel so much better about the tasks at hand, and at least for the moment that overthinking subsides. —
Joseph P., Indiana (Fitness Instructor)

Our opinion: This is another great example of taking a negative thought and turning it around to make you feel better. This is actually a tactic I have used with all three of my kids when they have a nightmare or negative thoughts before they go to bed. My middle child went through a phase when he was about 10 years old, where he would cry every single night lying in bed thinking that it was inevitable that my husband and I were going to pass away, and he would not have us around anymore. This topic was hard for me because I didn't want to lie to him and try to convince him it was not a big deal or downplay the way he felt, but I also didn't want to keep the conversation going too long to make the thoughts even more real and worse. So instead of replaying the negative thoughts I would turn the conversation around and have him think about something coming up in the future that was positive. That weekend was soccer tournaments, or we were going camping in a few days; even something a little more simple like "think about what you want your birthday theme to be this year." Giving him something to replace the negative thoughts helped him a lot, and he was able to learn to do this himself and shift his negative thoughts to keep himself from overthinking the sad and scary things in life.

Take a break with nature – I find the best solution for me when I am to the point of mental exhaustion is to simply take a walk outdoors. I will walk around the building on my lunch break at the office, or I will drive to the park near my home. Being outdoors, breathing

in the fresh clean air, helps me not only relax but re-energize. When I get back from my walks, I always feel ready to get back at it.
—James Z., West Virginia (Office Manager)

Our opinion: This is why running or walking can be such a great way to not only get some steps in but to also relax. There is nothing better than getting in a breath of fresh air to make you feel calm. Enjoying the world as it is, no drama, no chaos, just being. Getting completely away from technology and appreciating the world around you can help you realize that most of the things you tend to worry about are not nearly as big as you may think they are. You are still here, still a part of this world, and still able to make your life the way you really want it to be.

Dance it out – I find that dancing to my favorite songs help me relieve built up tension and stress that tend to cause my overthinking. When I'm nearing my breaking point, I will throw on my playlist and groove to the music until I am sweating profusely. This helps me relieve the anxiety and definitely gets my mind off the topic that was troubling me.
—Jennifer P., Pennsylvania (Medical Assistant)

Our opinion: There is nothing better than jumping around to some good music. Music is actually a great tool to calm the nerves and boost your mood. Did you know that some therapists will use music in their sessions because it is so powerful helping all types of mental and physical illnesses?

Ask yourself what's the worst that can happen! – To stop myself from always feeling overwhelmed and overthinking everything, I found a way to really connect myself to the issue and what it means. Start with 'What's the worst that can happen?' Figure out the answer to that question and then make a plan, even a back-up plan, to keep in place if the worst were to happen. (You will notice the worst probably isn't even all that bad.) Then make yourself a checklist of things to do in order to tackle the plan and then just do it, without multitasking or going in tons of directions. Take your problem one step at a time and get through it.
—Simon T., New York (Accountant)

Our opinion: This is another good example of making yourself take your thoughts step by step. This is also a great way to get yourself to really see the "big picture." Let's go back to the slipping and falling incident. The slip and fall happened a week ago, and you are okay so that means no physical injury occurred (that should be priority #1). Next, if your date is still talking to you then that means it didn't ruin your relationship (priority #2). If you are no longer dating that person, I'm seriously hoping it was not a break up created by a fall. Finally, even though it was extremely embarrassing at the moment, the moment has passed; it's not replaying on all the big screens at your local clubs. Once you walk yourself through all of these steps, you are likely to realize that you have been putting too much thought into this incident and it was not as big of a deal as you made it out to be.

Taking root – I like to connect myself physically and literally to the earth whenever I am in a whirlwind of thoughts and emotions. I put my toes into the soil and imagine that I am a tree or a plant with no worries or problems. My only reason for being is to grow and be.
—Naudia, Massachusetts (Yoga Instructor)

Our opinion: Connecting to the earth is one of the best ways to release tension and begin to let negative energy expel from your body. Learning how to ground yourself properly can be one of the best life-changing techniques you can use when you're starting to feel lost in the world. This is not just my opinion. There are many people around the world who swear by grounding or "earthing" themselves and practice it often.

(See our previous chapter on grounding.)

Imagine the worst-case scenario – When I find I have a negative thought spiraling out of control, I face it head on. I will ask myself: So, what if that situation were to really occur? What exactly is the worst that could happen to me? I will then determine the worst possible answer, and then solve it in my head. This way I am prepared for the very worst and the thought goes away.
—Michelle T., Pennsylvania (Occupational Therapist)

Our opinion: My thoughts and feelings are very torn on this one. I believe the idea of saying "what if" may lead some people down a rabbit hole of so many other negative thoughts and outcomes—giving your brain a chance to not only validate the fears you already have, but now giving yourself time to really think it out and quite possibly find even more scary scenarios you haven't even considered previously.

Listen to a good self-help audio book or podcast – When times get hard, I tend to turn to others for help. I listen to a self-help audio book or a good pick-me-up podcast. I turn my attention to something else that interests me and distracts me from any other thoughts that are not productive. I won't give in to worry about things that I cannot control so overthinking is something I can easily tap into and rid myself of.

—Sonya P., Massachusetts (Publisher)

Our opinion: This has been mentioned many times in this book. "Do not worry about the things you cannot control," but there is no statement more powerful than this one when it comes to overthinking and allowing negative thoughts to take over your mind. Also, drowning out these thoughts is another useful way to get through the negative cycle that swirls around in your head. Listening to a podcast of an audio book will help you interrupt the thoughts and pull them into another direction.

I'm sure you have realized by now my fascinations lie in the true crime world. When I am overly stressed out or my mind is recycling through the long list of negative thoughts I have accumulated over the week, I grab my favorite pair of noise-canceling headphones, turn on one of my true crime podcasts, and I take my dogs for a walk or clean the house. I get myself lost in a case and let go of everything that has been bothering me. This is also a great way to redirect your obsession and need to think things through. Getting lost in a mystery can help you focus on the details of the case and give you techniques for problem solving. It may also be a good way for you to realize your problems could be worse.

Conclusion

I am not perfect; I am not even a professional. I have a bachelor's degree in a field I don't even work in, and it has nothing to do with self-help, therapy, mental health, or any other topic this book has been written about. I didn't have to have a special education or a college degree to teach you lessons that I have experienced myself. The journey I have walked through for so many years has given me so much knowledge and insight on how learning to let go of the bad and embrace the good will pull you from some of the darkest places.

Despite how it sounded in the book, I do not hold any negative feelings toward my previous boss. I don't blame him for the feelings I held for months after I left the office, or even the mental struggles while I was there. What I learned so far in life is that I make it become what I want it to be. I chose to mope after being let go, I chose to work extra and stay at the job which caused me to break. In the end, it was my choices that got me to where I am today. And I am so glad for every choice I made. Good, bad, hard, painful. All my choices and all my struggles put me into a position to really have to challenge myself. I had to dig deeper than ever before to come out on the other side. I now realize I have the strength to do just about anything thrown at me, and I can be successful at it.

I can help my husband through his hard times, just like he stuck with me through mine. We have learned to cope together, live together, and heal each other. We have figured out how to tell when one of us is struggling, and what we can do to help each other through it. We have also figured out how to back off when it's something the other has to do on their own.

It may be a hard concept to accept for everyone, but you are not perfect, you were never perfect, and you will never be perfect. None of us are. Not Oprah, or the Pope, or even Beyonce herself. Everyone has flaws, everyone has self-doubt, and everyone has moments of regret. Whether you have what it takes to get through this or not is what separates us.

People who are willing to accept their flaws and work on themselves the best they can are the ones who seem like they have their life together all the time. But what you see on the outside can be very deceiving. This world has been chaotic for everyone these days, and no matter where you live, who you are, or the things you are suffering from, like a worldwide pandemic, political controversy, brutal weather, etc., you cannot escape, and you can't fix it either. You have to learn how to roll with the punches and get through life the best you can without losing yourself in the mess.

Spend time with your family, share memories with your kids, create memories they can one day share with their kids, and stop letting your mind keep you from living the life you have always dreamed of having. No one can help you with this, it's all on you. You have to be willing to get uncomfortable and face the fears that you have been letting control your entire life. Once you do this you will feel free, released from the pressure and pain of these recurring thoughts and negative feelings. Today is the day you improve your life and let go of everything that doesn't really matter. You have to put yourself first because no one else will.

www.ingramcontent.com/pod-product-compliance
Lightning Source LLC
Chambersburg PA
CBHW071452070526
44578CB00001B/321